me-T@iling

Published by **The Bowerdean Publishing Company Ltd.**
of 8 Abbotstone Road, London SW15 1QR

First published in 2000

© Tim Phillips

Tim Phillips has asserted his right under the Copyright,
Designs and Patents Act, 1988, to be identified
as Author of this Work.

All rights reserved.

No part of this publication may be reproduced, stored in a
retrieval system or transmitted in any form or by any means,
electronic, mechanical, photocopying, recording or otherwise
except brief extracts for the purpose of review, without
prior written permission of the publishers.

British Library Cataloguing-in-Publication Data.
A catalogue record for this book is available
from the British Library.

Designed by the Senate

Printed by Ashford Colour Press Ltd, Hampshire.

ISBN 0 906097 55 X

me-T@iling

How to help your **customers** help themselves

Tim Phillips

Sponsored by ReD retail decisions

BOWERDEAN
Publishing Company Limited

contents

1 Introduction
Why self-service exists, what it can do already, and why it's
the biggest challenge to customer relationships we have seen   **1**

2 Self service is not a fad
If you think self-service is a niche, you're wrong. There aren't
many businesses that it will not touch in the near future   **7**

3 Cook a fish, don't boil the ocean
Self-service in the traditional retail sector – how
to make it painless and profitable.   **18**

4 Distance no object
The call centre in the 21st century – why your phone customers
might prefer self-service, and how to treat them if they do   **28**

5 Have we met?
Knowing your customers if you never meet them – personalizing
your service and giving them what they want   **41**

6 More bright ideas
Self-service at the bleeding edge of business – new applications,
new channels, new ways to do business with your suppliers –
and what traditional businesses should learn from the dot-coms   **54**

7 Danger – card not present
Identifying and stopping fraud from your self-service customers.
The risks if you don't – and the rewards if you do   **66**

8 Where do we go from here?
Ten practical things you can do to make self-service work
for you if you're in business today   **83**

Helping yourself

You might not want to read the whole book (although we'd like you to). You can read it in order, or go straight to the chapters that are the most relevant, and read the rest when you have the time. So here's a quick self-service guide to where you can start, if you're just dipping into the book.

If you want to:

Start a new business
1 Introduction
2 Self-service is not a fad
6 More bright ideas

Rejuvenate a traditional business
3 Cook a fish, don't boil the ocean
5 Have we met?
8 Where do we go from here

Work out why your self-service application isn't paying for itself
7 Danger – card not present
8 Where do we go from here?

Convince your boss that self-service works
1 Introduction
2 Self service is not a fad

Convince your employees that self-service works
2 Self-service is not a fad
3 Cook a fish, don't boil the ocean
6 More bright ideas

CHAPTER 1
introduction

Today I remembered to order the shopping. Actually, my fridge reminded me. It has been keeping tabs on what I eat thanks to a bar-code reader on the door (life is too short to count the grams of saturated fat yourself). After my fridge called the supermarket on the Internet and placed my grocery order for me, which I have asked it to do every time I run out of low-fat essentials, I paid a couple of bills by putting them in my microwave oven. I went to the bank, or more precisely the ATM (that's all that's left of my local branch). After I keyed in my number, it reminded me that it's my niece's birthday and I had said I would order the home computer she's been promised by her parents, so I used the ATM to buy a tube ticket to the shops. And, of course, she was coming for tea, a fact my fridge had apparently forgotten to mention to me.

Off I went to my local supermarket. I was running late – so I grabbed a scanner on the way in and scanned the bar-codes on my own shopping as I raced round the aisles. This time I had remembered to bring my loyalty card, which has become very useful because, as a regular shopper, I get cheaper prices when I swipe my loyalty card and take a self-service trolley.

Then to lunch, where I picked my meal using an electronic menu on the table and swiped my Switch card to pay for it. Finally, to our local computer dealer, where I configured my niece's home computer using a touch-sensitive screen to tell the backroom staff what features I wanted. Picking it up at the exit, I had just enough time to get home before my low-fat groceries arrived. This was after making a stop at the travel agent on the way, of course, where I used another

me-t@iling

touch-screen terminal to pick my holiday destination, book my hotel room and get a discount flight. By the time my niece arrived, I was more than happy to see her. After all, although I'd done my grocery shopping, monitored my diet, paid my electricity bill, visited the bank, gone to lunch, bought and configured a computer, and booked my holiday, at the end of a busy day's shopping I hadn't spoken to a single person.

This is the science-fiction world of self-service retailing. Actually, it's no fiction. Everything we've talked about so far exists: sometimes in the laboratory, but often in real life. The microwave that pays your bills is still stuck in the laboratory at NCR, although its ATMs that can tell you your niece's birthday exist already, waiting for the banks that have installed them to write the applications to exploit the technology. Thousands of shoppers scan their own groceries every week at my local Safeway and have been doing so for several years. Do-it-yourself computers are the norm in 354 shops run by Best Buy, the USA's largest electronics retail chain but, closer to home, you can do exactly the same when you go to the web page of Dell Computer.

As I write, Virgin's self-service travel agent is being built in the Blade-Runner surroundings of Watford high street. When you enter this new world of self-service retailing, the conventional assumptions of how retailing works are turned upside down. Your customers tell you what they want, rather than being told by you what you can give them. Your customers decide when and how they want to do business with you, and your challenge is to give them the same facilities, no matter how they decide to shop. Self-service isn't just providing a new channel — it's about thinking of your customers in a more flexible way. It makes retailers work harder: if you are selling, you can no longer impose a single sales process on your customers. For companies which have struggled to cope with the call-centre revolution of the last ten years, the bad news is that the changes in retailing are just beginning.

"Many companies we work with assume customers always want to call the call centre," says Cap Gemini's head of customer relationship management (CRM) Caroline Mansley, whose customers have included Virgin Trains and BT Cellnet. "Your best customers will want a variety of channels and want the same standard of service in each. For example, in banking it's great to use a call centre, it's fantastic to use an on-line bank and it's wonderful to use an ATM. But banks have provided only some services on some channels, and customers now demand the same service across all of them."

think positive

It seems impossible to provide good service through self-service: surely, you say, it's all about saving a retailer's time and money. That's the way that we have been brought up to think of self-service: the battered vending machine, the curly sandwich in the cafeteria. It is a culture of the lowest common denominator: convenience shopping for those who can, or have to, put up with it. Yet we'll see that not only can retailers use self-service to improve the customer experience, but that customers now expect self-service to be a positive experience, offering all the comforts of their traditional shopping. Ultimately, self-service shopping can become the retail channel that most of your customers choose, not necessarily because it is quick, or because it is cheap, but because it gives them confidence and a high level of service that has largely disappeared in some retailing experiences.

If this sounds ridiculous, recall the last time you were caught in a never-ending telephone queue to buy a plane ticket. (If you can't, take it from me, such queues exist.) United Airlines has supplemented its call centres with an automated telephone ticket-booking system which uses a computer system to recognize customers' speech and figure out which destinations and types of tickets they are asking for. It will complete the transaction by taking and processing a credit card number and delivering these tickets without asking the customers to talk to any of its staff. After the system has been in operation one year, more than 50 per cent of its telephone customers say they prefer to buy tickets this way.

me-t@iling

In this book, we're going to look at the opportunities in self-service retailing: how it changes traditional retail environments, how thinking strategically about self-service can make call centres, mail order and web pages work better. We will see how self-service takes cost out of some parts of your business.

Take call centres as an example. Gartner Group calculates that 56 per cent of the cost of running a call centre is spent on paying the people inside it. Another 18 per cent is spent on training these humans so they are ready to talk to your customers. Properly done, replacing these humans with self-service computer software that recognizes what your customers say, can actually increase the amount of business that you do while cutting these costs. We will see how self-service broadens your horizons. There's a limited advantage in being able to sell the same number of items at half the cost. There's a much bigger advantage in selling twice as many items with no increase in overheads. We will also see how these changes open up new opportunities for radical self-service, retail ideas like reverse auctions and buyers' clubs, that might fundamentally change the way you do business. Ideas that even a few years ago would at best have caused a snigger around the boardroom table are now being embraced by such radical organizations as General Motors.

Think of the examples above: we have ATMs that sell tickets or supermarket trolleys that control what price we have to pay. We have fridges that monitor our diet and automatically make up an order based on the parameters that we have chosen. Sometimes self-service opportunities are simple. I'd like a service where I could ask the bank to remind me of family birthdays. It's in the bank's interest to remind me, because it could help me draw the right amount of cash. The technology is there to do it – so why doesn't it work? The answer is that we're not used to selling this way. The ATM has always been a 'lowest common denominator' device, good for the basic functions, nothing more. It comes from a time when the bank was still a building which held on to your money for you. Today, banks want to be centres of financial management – but they're missing a trick if they don't extend that to cover their main interface with their customers – the 25,000 ATMs that are responsible for two billion cash withdrawals every year in the UK alone. It's easy to beat up on the banks, but almost every retailer has an opportunity to use self-service to make customers happier.

risks

But we will also look at the risks of self-service. Self-service customers have control in a way that changes your business model profoundly. Your customers can just hang up or drift away. For example, unless your web page is easy to navigate, most of your customers will never consummate the purchase they are considering. (Research shows that even successes like Amazon.com could multiply sales by ten overnight if only everyone who put a book into the 'shopping basket' actually bought it, instead of ducking out at the last minute.) The relative anonymity of self-service also adds risk to your business. How do we know that shoppers who scan their own food are scanning everything in the basket? How do we know the credit card number that your IVR (interactive voice recognition) telephone system is being given is genuine? As a retailer, you bear the risk of card-not-present transactions, not the bank. If the card is being used fraudulently, you pay that cost. With card-not-present fraud booming, it can be a high price to pay for innovation

Evidence also suggests that fraudsters will quickly find weak links and expose them. If your self-service strategy isn't properly planned, your fraud losses will not just climb slightly – you'll take on all the shrinkage losses that your competitors were suffering. A poorly planned self-service idea isn't just a way to get rid of good customers, it will also attract bad ones. Ultimately, as a result either of the opportunities or the risks, self-service retailing has the ability to tell you what the real value is in what you sell.

Is your customer service fundamentally about smiling, and are those smiles an attempt to conceal the deficiencies in what you are really offering? We'll meet companies that found out uncomfortable truths

me-t@iling

about what they thought was customer service and discovered late in the day what sort of service their customers really wanted. Self-service exposes how much, or how little, you really know about your customers and forces you to use and collect that information more effectively. It tells you where the holes are in your security and how those holes should be filled – because, if you don't fill them quickly, you're literally telling fraudsters to 'help themselves'. And it asks you whether the business that you are running today has the fundamental strength to be a successful business tomorrow, because, without doubt, this will be a decade of self-service.

It's brave to stand up and say, "We know what our customers want from us." It's a lot braver to say, "We're going to test that by letting them pick what they want from us." Perhaps it is bravest of all to say, "We put this to the test, and our customers are telling us that everything we thought about service was wrong, and now we are going to change it."

It was put more succinctly by one American executive, introducing his self-service telephone ordering system to the British market. "Our customers taught us a lot of lessons about what we weren't doing, and how we covered that up. So from now on, our software will never, ever tell you to Have A Nico Day."

CHAPTER 2
self-service is not a fad

What is self-service? It's letting customers come to you, decide what they will buy, then giving them a machine for making the purchase – a machine that they operate themselves. The 'machine' isn't important: it can be a vending machine, a set of shelves to browse along, a web site's database of items for sale seen on the Internet, or a bank's central computer systems through an ATM. The way your customer operates this machine can be just as varied. Customers may have to swipe cards, make sounds for a computer to recognize, press buttons. What matters is that the retailer builds a system and gives it to the customer to use with no assistance necessary, or so all concerned hope. If the customer can't make the retailer's self-service machine work or if the customer doesn't want to make it work, then the sale doesn't occur. And why do customers want to work the machine? Traditionally because retailers have made it worth their while.

Robin Bloor, the author of *The Electronic Economy*, views the birth of self-service as a fundamental shift in the retailer–customer relationship: 'The supermarket was a phenomenon of the 1950s, which has increased with sophistication with the passage of time. The retailing mechanism can be viewed as an outsourcing arrangement – the retailer outsources the picking of goods and the economic benefit of this is shared with the customer by virtue of lower prices.'

Self-service is nothing new. Retail customers have been helping themselves by filling up their trolleys in supermarkets for half a century. Cafeterias have been around just as long. Mail-order

me-t@iling

catalogues – the machine is the catalogue's system of classifying the items for sale, the action is filling in a form to order them – have been around for just as long. Banks have been using ATMs in the UK for more than twenty years, and withdrawals from ATMs now outnumber over-the-counter transactions by three to one. We're not about to argue the point that self-service exists, as it plainly does, even if it's rarely thought about as a sales channel on a par with traditional retailing. But, before we get into the details of self-service today, we need to squash the image of it as an unfortunate necessity, to get beyond the idea that it's a dirty job, but someone has to do it – and that someone is the poor customer, because he or she has been bribed.

Certainly a financial incentive is always useful to create demand. But it is not the only driver behind self-service. There's a larger shift in attitude among customers. To find out how today's self-service world has evolved, it's not enough to look at what retailers are attempting to provide. So the first point to make is that self-service has to exist and will continue to grow, whether the financial rewards are increased or not. The second point is that self-service is not just one option among many for growing a retail business in the Internet economy. It is the only viable option. If both these principles are true, then retailers who ignore self-service, or pay lip-service to it, are letting down not only their customers but their shareholders too. And that's just the situation today – next month, or next year, the stakes will be much higher. The reward for taking self-service seriously in 2005? You get to keep your job.

hit or myth?

First, where does this public demand stem from? Let's examine a few myths about customer demand. First, there is the myth that the customer always wants to talk to a real person: the idea which has spawned the job of 'shop greeter' - the person who stands at the door and hopes we "have a good day". A recent survey concluded that 50 per cent of Americans – yes, Americans – consider themselves 'shy', and prefer to avoid human contact when they can.

The result? They like to use machines because they don't particularly enjoy talking to real people. One can only imagine the horror that a large proportion of the shopping public experiences when greeted by someone whose only job is to talk to them, whether they like it or not. Whether this statistic is the sign of a healthy society isn't our business at the moment. What's indisputably true is that there is a group of people who like to use a type of retailing that doesn't imply gratuitous personal contact.

Here is an example closer to home. British Telecom conducted a survey into how customers wanted to communicate with telephone banks. Although for some functions, most preferred to talk to call-centre agents, the majority would love a self-service option when it came to awkward or embarrassing requests – for example, applying for an overdraft. This doesn't mean the bank has to give all these customers an overdraft – there's no reason why the criteria should change at all. It doesn't mean that in problem cases those customers can't be funnelled back to a live agent. But for the vast majority of short-term small-scale borrowing requirements, customers would relish the chance to help themselves.

Shyness, embarrassment and social awkwardness aren't recent inventions. They have always been with us. But if half the population counts itself as shy, then this might be half a population that's worth listening to. If you're a retailer who wants to make that half of the population happy, you might want to give them the opportunity to serve themselves. You might be wondering why we haven't heard more about this before. Don't think, 'no one ever asked me.' They wouldn't, would they? They are shy.

Another myth is that shoppers won't want self-service unless it's forced on them. We're a population whose shopping habits are changing. Last year, NOP conducted a survey of British buying habits. Already, two out of five of us are perfectly happy to buy goods over a telephone rather than in person, and half of us said we're happy to do that in future. This is a new way to shop, but not

me-t@iling

necessarily self-service. But 7 per cent of us said we're happy to buy over the net, with 36 per cent happy to do it in the future — and web shopping is, by its nature, self-service from beginning to end.

Let's look at those results in context. At the time the survey was completed, more British people said they would be happy to buy over the Internet than actually had access to it. It's probably fair to say that what drives many users to get Internet access is the possibility of shopping. This is not the profile of a customer base that has to be force-fed with self-service.

Myth number three is that history shows us that people are put off by self-service technology. In that last survey, the proportion of the population that's happy to buy over the phone and the proportion that's happy to use self-service aren't very different. Considering the spectacular growth of the call centre business (40 per cent a year, according to the Call Centre Association), this is an amazing change in three years. Although many retailers have embraced the call-centre revolution, these call centres are not commonly set up to help self-service shoppers, either on the Internet or over the telephone — not yet. We'll cover why not and what is to be done in the future in more detail later in the book. All we're saying at the moment is that demand is there already. This leads us on to another myth — that there's plenty of time to get self-service right.

This argument says that if we have been meddling with the principle for half a century to get to where we are now, then we should be good for another, oh, 150 years. By which time many of us will have retired. But there is also evidence that when markets switch to self-service, they do so with an astonishing rapidity. Today, more than half the mobile phones in the UK use a pay-as-you-go model, barely two years after it was introduced. Prepay mobile telephones are a pure self-service application. Instead of forcing customers to endure a credit check, a waiting period, a subscription charge and a minimum payment, the customers have the choice to serve themselves and buy telephone time when, and if, they need it. Again, we'll cover this in more detail later in the book, but at this point the only thing we need to know is that telephone companies that weren't ahead of this market immediately found themselves behind it. In the self-service world, vendors are either early or late, never on time.

Here's another example. At the beginning of the year 2000, one in ten share purchases on the London stock exchange was done over the Internet. This business is switching to the net at a rate of approximately 2 per cent every month. Being a stockbroker is perhaps the most endangered retailer's job there is.

no escape

So far we have argued that the public demand for self-service is real, and is driven by many forces of which the chance to save cash is only the most visible. We have argued that the appetite for self-service technologies, particularly the Internet, has already been whetted, that consumers are well aware of the rules of the self-service game. We've seen two examples of customers putting those rules into practice and changing entire markets in a matter of months. Why then, looking at history, should we deduce that self-service is the only model for the future of many retailers?

First, because when these retailers need to expand their markets, self-service technologies represent a far cheaper way of doing it. Robin Bloor said that retailers have 'outsourced' the job of picking the goods for customers. That saves time, it saves money, and, now that we have the technology to make self-service into good service, these are not savings anyone can afford to ignore.

Second, building these 'machines' to help customers help themselves is the only practical way to deal with the demands that businesses, even 'steady state' businesses will face. The Internet, for example, expands a potential customer base into the millions. These customers will have questions, doubts and insecurities that need to be solved before they become real customers. One of Motorola's factories currently gets 4,000 customer contacts a day. It is

me-t@iling

expecting a growth in the next year to 70,000. You simply cannot take on enough people to handle these calls.

Third, you can disguise your self-service. Try e-mailing Abbey National and you will be astonished at how quickly you get a reply. This isn't because the company has thousands of mail answerers frantically typing replies. It is because Abbey National has a software program that sucks the meaning out of your question and composes a reply automatically for four out of five incoming mail messages. This is self-service disguised, but it's still self-service. Most of the time, the customer just doesn't know that he or she is operating the 'machine', which is a great incentive.

getting your retaliation in first

Your organization's ability to handle e-mail will be one of the tests of whether your current (for 'current' read 'obsolete') model of customer service still works. More than half of the UK's major retailers cannot reply to a mail message within 48 hours, so most are failing the test. But to view this only as a test of your ability to send e-mail is trivializing the issue. Now that you know that your Federal Express parcel is traceable thanks to its bar-code, you're tempted to find out where it is.

The ability to provide a service creates a demand for that service. If FedEx had restricted the use of the tracking service to personal callers only, the demand on the call centre would immediately have exploded. Instead, you can find out where your package is by going to the web site. Get the information yourself and it's a viable service. Rely on the company to provide it, and it's not.

There are any number of these services which can only be provided in a self-service environment. Cliff Condon, the research director at analyst Forrester Europe, identifies three trends that will change retailing completely. Forrester's name for the new economy is 'dynamic trade' – an environment in which many of the things which were fixed, like prices, are now flexible. "Dynamic trade is like a propeller that has three blades. The first principle is that services eclipse products. The second is that demand drives production. The third is that the pricing for your product or service matches market conditions," he says.

Let's take these in order. The services that you provide alongside your products become more important than the products themselves. At its most basic, a mobile phone handset has become a commodity device. What made the mobile market explode was the service provided around that handset — that is, the ability to control how much you spend on calls. Traditional improvements, such as a reduction in call costs, lighter handsets or wider coverage, have had a far smaller effect in this country. A more futuristic example is the washing machine that is guaranteed never to be broken. It can be built by engineering the parts to a much higher specification, or by building hundreds of service centres across the country. Both are traditional products, very expensive to supply. Instead, you can build a washing machine that monitors its own systems and is connected to the Internet.

"Why would the Internet be useful on a washing machine?" Condon asks, "So a manufacturer does not have to dispatch people to come and fix it of course." If the problem is not mechanical, it can be fixed using the Internet connection. If the problem is mechanical, the machine can automatically ask for a service — which may even be preventative maintenance. All we have to do now is work out how to squeeze a maintenance engineer down the telephone wire. The drive to provide greater levels of service has created 'service inflation'. Self-service is the only realistic route out in most cases.

The second principle, that demand drives production, raises the question 'Why build more than you can sell?' To which the answer is 'Because you have to'. Again, self-service gets us out of this historical problem. By letting customers drive production, you don't have to keep inventory. It's what Dell has done. It's what others will soon be doing. "How long will it be before you can order a tailor-made car and watch its manufacture over the Internet by virtue of cameras on the production line?" asks Robin Bloor, "Not long".

Whether customers want to watch their car being made or whether they are happy to stick with their regular television programmes, the system only works if you let the customer drive production directly. A retail system that puts intermediaries in the way loses many of the benefits that customer-driven production achieves. The trials of Compaq, Dell's main competitor, are an illustration of this. It has struggled to match Dell's price changes (every day), new product introductions (every week) and number of stock turns for a decade.

The last blade of Condon's dynamic trade propellor is variable pricing. Retailers need to adjust prices regularly (as Dell does, every day). To match your pricing to demand, you need instant information on what that demand actually is. Self-service technologies help this process in a profound way that we haven't seen before. A simple example is the most basic of self-service devices, a vending machine.

"The coolest things that I found in Finland were the drinks machines," says Condon. "If you have a mobile telephone, you push a button, and the charge for the can of Coke goes on to your phone bill. Now imagine it for one hot day of the year in Finland, and people are drinking Coca-Cola like crazy." The retailer incurs a cost if he has to refill the machine before it is completely empty — so why not give customers an incentive to drink something else? "Why not use the Internet to drop the pricing on your orangeade so that people will drink orangeade instead of Coke?" Condon explains.

tricky customers

Self-service offers another way out of a traditional problem: what to do with problem customers. These customers aren't necessarily the complainers. They are the ones that don't make you any profit. Self-service is a mechanism that can propel them towards becoming profitable once more. The retailer's message is 'Your incentive, dear customer, is that this is all the service you are going to get. If you don't like it, please go and affect another company's bottom line'. We don't say this, but we mean it. The customer's incentive is 'I get to stay as a customer'. Traditionally many retailers have ignored this issue. Time is running out. We've already mentioned the cost of running a call centre. This cost will go up.

An example is a company called Octane Software which supplies retailers with software to provide efficient customer service. Its customers have, in the last two years, acquired a completely new set of customer-service problems. It has seen an explosion in the number of customers that companies with a web site have to support – and the number of times those customers ask for support. And in the traditional environment, each support request loses the company money.

"Scalability in the traditional customer relationship management environment might mean being able to handle 10,000 calls a day. We have a customer who now has to handle 700,000 interactions every day. This is Internet scalability. Applications need to be able to cope with Internet scalability," says Jim Lambert, the director of corporate marketing.

The problem is how to tell the difference between good customers and bad, or in the argot, between 'oranges' and 'lemons'. Unless you go through this identification process, your self-service will be as bad as your ordinary service, because you have no idea who your customers are, never mind what they want. It's this lack of customer knowledge, he says, that is holding self-service back, but, ultimately, identifying your low-margin customers and pushing them towards self-service is the only way out. "If you can't support your customers properly, giving them another channel to see you fail is not progress."

As we look at the retail environment today, there is one massive motivator for self-service already in place: plastic. Credit and debit cards make it possible to buy and sell without being in the same location, or without having to wait in a queue, or without having to

me-t@iling

carry cash. We Brits love our cards: our credit-card terminals are more important than our tills. In the UK, there wasn't a single plastic card until 1966. Now there are 112 million of them — almost three for every adult, with the numbers still climbing.

In 1998, twice as many purchases were made with debit cards as with personal cheques. Since 1989, the number of cash purchases has been on a gentle downward curve — around 15.3 billion that year, to around 14 billion in 1998, according to the Association for Payment Clearing Services (APACS). In the same period, the number of cheques written has declined from almost 2.5 billion, to just over 2 billion. In the next ten years, the number of purchases that will be made using cards will double. What's driving this?

It's no surprise that the biggest growth area is card-not-present purchasing. Self-service will be a huge part of this trend. The more we look around us, the more we see that self-service isn't just a fad or a curiosity. It's a fundamental part of our retail experience already, and it's only going to become more important. Customers like it and retailers need it. It may cut costs, but it can also streamline service and help those retailers expand. In the future, it is likely to prove the cornerstone of most of the emerging sales channels. That's the future though. First, let's look in detail at how self-service works in today's retail world.

me-t@iling

graphs: transaction volumes in the UK (millions)

credit card purchases

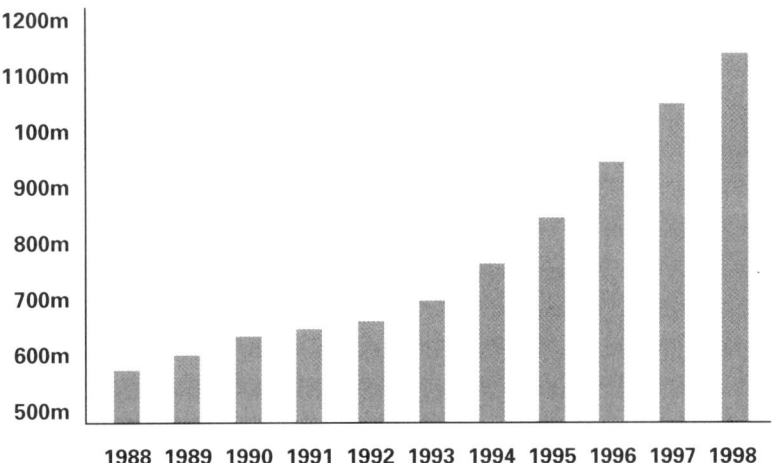

source: **APACS**

debit card purchases

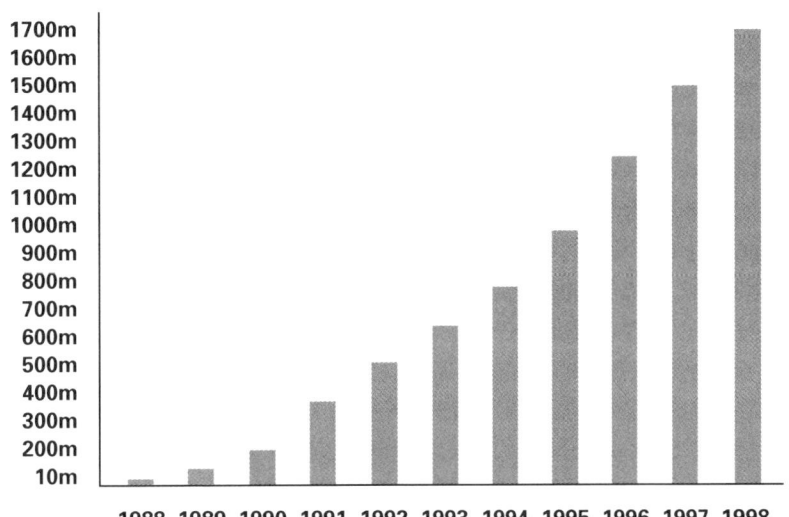

source: **APACS**

CHAPTER 3
cook a fish, don't boil the ocean

In other words, retailing doesn't have to be done the hard way when there's an alternative. In many cases, from video shops to courthouses, an alternative for the future of traditional retail can be provided by self-service. Questions like: 'how do we manage costs?', 'how do we personalize our service?' or 'how do we cut queues?' have many answers, most of which have worked or will work. Self-service isn't the only answer to these questions — but it is one answer, as we shall see.

It is also an answer that can cut much of the complexity out of these problems. Self-service is about building some type of machine that the customer operates. Automating this process can also take much of the error out of it while retaining more of the useful customer information needed for the future.

Furthermore, it's not rocket science, and it's all the better for it. Unless your customers can operate your self-service device, there's really no point in having it — unless you like annoying them.

But first, on a more personal level, I can confirm that as a customer, self-scanning in a supermarket works for me. I have five bags of shopping here, having shaved ten minutes off my personal best, to prove it.

Of course, Safeway would have been able to tell me this. In 171 stores in the UK — as well as in about 100 Sainsbury and Waitrose stores — self-scanning is old hat. Safeway has offered self-scanning in its stores since 1995, only a few years after electricity was invented, and several months before food retailing was revolutionized by the discovery of the kumquat.

For those of you who have yet to experience the kumquat, its flavour is tart, then sweet. Good-quality kumquats will be firm and bright orange. You eat the pips.

For those of you who have yet to experience self-scanning (700,000 shopping baskets a week and rising are self-scanned, so you may soon be an endangered species), here is how to do it. In Safeway, you insert your card to get access to a portable scanner, which is about the size of a water pistol. Using the scanner, you swipe items before they go into your basket. You then return your scanner to its slot, and retrieve a receipt, which you use to pay at a special self-scanner's checkout.

How does this work for your customer? Simple – it saves them time. They spend the same time shopping, but they don't have to queue.

happy customers

How does this work for Safeway? It gives them happy customers who don't have to queue. It reduces the number of people the company has to employ to sit at a checkout. It means that more of the store can be used to sell things, and less has to be used to process people and their baskets of shopping.

A BRMB survey of shopper attitudes in 1997 asked consumers what they wanted from supermarkets in the future. Just over 10 per cent said they would like a crèche or a dry cleaner. Double that figure wanted banking facilities. About a quarter wanted longer opening hours or home delivery. Most of these requirements have been delivered in the years that followed – indeed, topics like home delivery and supermarket banks have dominated the retail news agenda.

However, twice as many shoppers – almost half those surveyed – asked for something to be done about the length of time they spent

me-t@iling

in queues. Usually the supermarkets have responded to this by adding more checkout operators at busy times. But what do you do with those operators before and afterwards? Self-service has been relegated to the back seat. It's still viewed as a 'gee-whizz' idea by many retailers, perhaps good for a slot on *Tomorrow's World*, but a technology that creates more problems than it solves. When he was running Asda, Archie Norman decreed that none of his stores would ever use self-scanning. Considering that supermarkets were the first mass-market self-service idea this century, this might seem to be an odd promise to make. But, so far, Asda stores have kept their word.

Yet self-service supermarkets are already showing how, in practice, serving yourself can open new horizons. It's also beginning to show how quickly these projects can pay for themselves.

John Pellaumail is the man who put self-scanners on Safeway walls. He is the director of consumer systems for Symbol Technologies, who make the scanners and make sure that they work with the shop's retail systems. Often, in the last decade, his job has been unofficial cheerleader for self-scanning.

He identifies two factors that make self-scanning work. "If the retailers make the experience of shopping pleasant, then people now spend more with them. Second, because the experience has been good for customers, it means that they might only go to one store regularly, instead of shopping at two or three. Those customers will think twice about going to another store. They will be more loyal."

That's basic good sense, but no more compelling than running a set of special offers, or a loyalty card, or opening for longer hours. We can make this argument for many of the improvements that retailers have already made to the shopping experience.

Few improvements though have the ability to make the store work better as well. "I was talking to the supermarket manager recently, and he said to me: 'Twenty years ago I had five butchers and three bakers, today I have two butchers and one baker – the rest of the shop runs more efficiently as well'," says Pellaumail. "He said 'the only place that hasn't become more efficient is the front of the store. It's actually getting worse'." Today, checkout costs are about 25 per cent of the cost of running a supermarket.

the pay-off

Five years is enough time to gather data on which users like to self-scan, which ones get the most out of it, and whether the idea pays for itself – in short, whether it's a good idea. Safeways has seen some surprising results.

The first, and the most important day-to-day result is that users don't steal things. It's natural to imagine that when customers service themselves, they also help themselves. According to Pellaumail, Symbol's experience worldwide has shown the increase in shrinkage to be tiny. "Our customers can't measure the shrinkage from store to store. For a supermarket you're talking about 2 per cent for shrinkage. Any additional losses that they are getting from self-scanning are in the 'point zero zero' range."

His explanation is that consumers exert social pressure on themselves, and on each other. If the checkout operator scans your shopping, and accidentally doesn't charge you for a bottle of wine, that's the retailer's fault, and you don't feel obliged to go back and pay for it. But that's a lot different from dropping a bottle into the trolley, not scanning it on purpose, and walking out with it. The first is a mistake. The second is stealing.

Also, research in self-scanning supermarkets shows that consumers watch self-scanners closely. The explanation? They don't want their fellow shoppers 'ruining things' by abusing the system. To some extent, it is self-policing. The upshot is that Safeway has prosecuted two people in five years. Yet Symbol's greatest opposition comes from the security staff who are resisting what they consider to be anarchy. "When you meet the security guy, he's got his arms crossed-

he's saying to us 'there's no way you're coming into my store with that'," Pellaumail jokes.

The 'softer' consumer benefits of self-scanning are less obvious. "When you see retired people using it you might think 'Why?', they have lots of time to wait in the queue," says Pellaumail, "but they may use it because they are on a budget. They don't have to experience 'checkout shock' – the 'oh my God' moment at the checkout." Because they can find out the cost of their groceries at any time, self-scanning is a safety net, a bonus service.

Customers have also said they prefer self-scanning because they know the price on the shelf is the real price. And when there's a discrepancy, the supermarket's staff can be sure that some customer will point it out right away.

Who's to say you can't provide different prices for different shoppers? One supermarket in the USA already uses five separate price bands for self-scanners: regular shoppers pay less. If your customers identify themselves with a loyalty card, then a system of automatic discounts isn't impossible. This is a three-pronged incentive: you're increasing loyalty, you're cutting the cost of administering the loyalty card reward system, and you're driving customers to self-scanning by offering a discount.

This chapter is about the traditional retail environment and we're going to pretend that the Internet doesn't exist, because it doesn't for most people. No matter how popular shopping for groceries over the net becomes, there will still be a need for retail premises for shoppers who prefer not to use it. Their requirements may soon change though. If you are comparing self-scanning with queuing, then self-scanning is quicker. If you are comparing a supermarket with a web site, then you don't have to queue at all at the web site. So, unless the supermarket has queue-avoidance strategies, traditional retailers might soon look as if they are punishing shoppers for visiting their shops!

me-t@iling

What's in it for the retailers, apart from these grandiose schemes of multiple pricing and loyalty discounts? Quite a lot, according to a report from Dresdner Kleinwort Benson Research. Here are the headlines:

- Self-scanning increases the size of a shopping basket by between 10 and 15 per cent.

- Around one in four baskets is self-scanned as soon as the technology is introduced. That means if a store runs 24 checkouts, it only has to run 18 afterwards – at most.

- The cost of self-scanning for 150 stores is £30 million.

- Self-scanning is a cost in year one – but by year two, it's already a profit for the supermarket.

The report concludes that whatever use is made of self-scanning technology, there's a benefit. Even if that benefit is from redeploying shop staff elsewhere – as Safeway has done – payback can come inside two years. But at that point, there's the chance to move on, add new functionality to the self-service concept. Staff have been trained in other disciplines, data about self-service customers has been acquired. It's effectively a free experiment, even if self-service never becomes more than an interesting niche.

But self-service answers some of the fundamental questions that retailers will be faced with in the near future. On the one hand, it will drive loyalty and increase service among a group of customers. On the other hand, it will solve some of the problems that customers will never see.

problem solved

One of these is the competition for new sites. Tighter planning restrictions plus a lack of easily obtainable city centre locations will

me-t@iling

increase the importance of this issue. Self-service can increase the efficiency of a site – so town-centre convenience shopping becomes more convenient. Verdict Research says that 'The race for space of the 1980s, when physical growth [for retailers] was over 3 per cent per annum, will not be repeated under the current planning regulations.' Instead, that growth will be nearer 1 per cent, and the biggest growth won't be in the out-of-town 'big sheds', with room for as many checkouts as the retailer needs. It will be in the high street.

But the growth in the amount customers spend in those supermarkets will be nearer 3 per cent. The retail premises will have to become more space-efficient.

A new generation of shopping trolleys (IBM and ICL both have versions) goes further – by showing users the discounts that are available in the aisle they are visiting, or by directing them to the items they have decided they want to buy. "If a user scans pasta, we can make recommendations as to which sauces they might care to try," says Mike Winch, the IT director at Safeway, which is trying out the idea. Rather grandly, Safeway calls this a 'virtual shop assistant'.

So far we have concentrated on the supermarket shopping experience, because it's one of the highest-profile areas in which self-service has made an impact. But it is by no means the only one. Go through the doors of Heathrow Terminal One and turn right. On your right, there's a check-in. It's the one without a queue of bored-looking people. Actually, there's no-one there at all, apart from the occasional British Airways helper, who stays in the background. The self-service check-in is a group of hefty-looking kiosks into one of which you post your ticket. It then lets you pick your seat and prints your boarding pass, leaving you standing there, thinking: 'Is that it then?'

Indeed it is.

BA has allocated its self-service check-in desks so that those of us who don't have three suitcases and a steamer trunk and who would otherwise be condemned to stand at the back of the check-in queue thinking 'What do people at airline check-in desks have to talk about that takes fifteen minutes?' have an alternative that makes us feel better about entering an airport.

The BA self-service check-in exists for one reason: to manage queues. But for customers, it is a liberating experience far more important than simply avoiding a five-minute wait. It means they can manage their own time, knowing that, when they turn up to an airport, they are unlikely to have an unexpected wait.

But BA's self-service kiosks show some of the practical problems and challenges of self-service. The first is that while it's good for Terminal One, the home of short-haul flying, where many customers carry a briefcase and little else, it's almost impossible to design a machine that will check a steamer trunk in Terminal Four, where many of the passengers will be flying halfway around the world. And even if they did, would customers feel safe checking their own bags? Many of us would be prepared to queue for fifteen minutes, because the thirty seconds of interaction we have at the end of that wait eases our airport anxiety, and we feel (wrongly in some cases) that it is a way to stop our bags landing in Stockholm at the time we are landing in Sydney.

don't be shy

So, on the one hand, self-service has to be targeted at those who can, and will, use it. But self-service also has to be given the opportunity to work. Five years ago, Boots unsuccessfully tried a self-service information kiosk. Hardly anyone used the pilot version. When the designer went to find out what the problem was, he found the kiosk tucked away at the back of the shop. "We needed to keep it out of people's way," the shop manager said.

The project was doomed to fail – not just because many customers who might have used the kiosk had no idea it existed, even when they were standing two metres away – but also because of the

me-t@iling

message it sent about the retailer's commitment to self-service. It said, 'We are embarrassed about this', 'It's not really for you', or worse, 'This has nothing to do with our business'. Customers who don't use technology when these are the messages being sent out aren't ignoring self-service. They are taking the retailer's hint not to use it.

Similarly, BA's first self-service kiosks were hidden in a cubbyhole. Customers looked on confused. Its latest version is smack in front of you as you run to the check-in desk – if you don't want to use it, you might still trip over it.

To make a success, self-service has to be presented without embarrassment, and as a simple alternative. Once you do that, it's surprising how readily retailers can change customer attitudes.

Do you want to hire a video tonight? You can go and browse in the store, but, chances are that you know exactly which video you want, so why not use a vending machine to get it, rather than wandering around the store and standing in the queue? Blockbuster knows that the value in what it provides to regular customers isn't the chance to meet the checkout operator. It is getting them home to watch the film they want before the dinner burns.

If you're living in Phoenix, Arizona, and you want to get home in time to watch your video, but you have to file for divorce first, then pop into the City's Maricopa County Self-Service Legal Center and fill the forms in yourself using the special guidance that the Courthouse offers. It's fair to say that civil court actions are a retail business run by solicitors. For four years, the residents of Phoenix have had the chance to do the job themselves, because the City took the initiative and told them that they could.

All the above examples have one thing in common: they exist to strip complexity out of basic processes. We've over-complicated some retail tasks in a way that no longer suits customers and obscures the real value of the transaction.

ask the customer

But there's one final point to make. If we want to find out what customers want, there's no finer way than self-service. Because self-service gives any customer the ability to pick exactly what they want from you, that is what they will tend to do. This can be very powerful. For example, today, if you use your Advantage loyalty card in Boots, you'll be aware that its shops have kiosks into which you can insert your card, allowing you to pick out what you want to use your loyalty points to get a discount on. It's almost literally a way to print money. Customers don't have to wait for their loyalty to be rewarded by a form letter containing half a dozen coupons for bizarre products they'd never dream of buying, because that's what their loyalty card issuer thinks they want. Or wants them to want.

On the one hand, this is self-service in a basic form – it's a simple kiosk (note that, this time, they've stuck them right in the middle of the store) but it is also a powerful way to analyse customer demand. If you want to work out what discounts your customers would like, the route many retailers have taken through the 1990s is to collect all the customer data, analyse it, segment the customers, run focus groups, analyse the findings, map to their current range and compare with existing buying decisions.

Boots stick a kiosk in the middle of a shop and see what the customers ask for, then provide more of it. Ask the customer: it's an old-fashioned concept in retailing, but one that's just as good today as it ever was – and now you can ask the customer without having to employ real human beings to do it. With simple self-service concepts like this one, it's possible to rediscover the sort of customer service that many retailers have lost.

Self-service tells retailers immediately what customers want and gives them a chance to act on it directly and cheaply. Why do this the hard way? As the saying goes, 'Cook a fish, don't boil the ocean'.

CHAPTER 4
distance no object

A bank customer from Roanoke in Virginia, USA, called his bank a few months ago to complain. Actually he wrote a computer program to keep calling eight branches of his bank. When the bank answered, the program left a message: 'This is an automated customer complaint. To hear a live complaint, press button one.' When the bank employee pressed one, he or she heard 'The customer is unable to come to the phone right now, but your call is very important. Thank you for being patient.'

If self-service is a niche in the face-to-face retail world, it's much more common over the telephone or the Internet. The call centre lends itself to self-service well. The World-Wide Web makes self-service the standard way to shop.

The problem is that too many retailers are using self-service to give their customers a hard time. Next time you're stuck in a phone queue, waiting to press one to go round a loop for the third time, remember that God helps those who help themselves – and God help those who don't.

In this chapter we'll look at why these two media, the telephone and the Internet, are such useful engines for self-service, and at what are the possibilities for generating huge amounts of business when you start them. But we'll also be showing the destructive effect of poorly planned, poorly realised self-service applications, a category which, sadly, includes far too many examples.

call centres

The call-centre revolution is over: the call centres won. They already employ 1.5 per cent of the working population in the UK, with that figure set to double in the next few years. That's already a greater proportion of the population than used to work in the mines. The demand for call centres is growing at between 30 and 40 per cent per year.

Yet it's not hard to find someone who has a call-centre horror story. You, for example, probably have at least one.

Self-service technology has to take much of the blame for this. Interactive Voice Recognition, or IVR in the jargon, is the most obvious and pervasive example of self-service technology to have emerged in the last decade. Today it's almost impossible to buy a cinema ticket without having to do battle with it, and it's being used everywhere from share dealing to exam grading.

IVR comes in several flavours. There's tone recognition, where you press '1' to speak to a sales representative, '2' to listen to hold music, '3' to hear this again. There's the glamorously titled 'grunt' recognition, where you have to make a noise at the right time – any noise. And there is fully fledged voice recognition, where the software recognizes – or attempts to recognize – exactly what you are asking.

It's a technology-heavy area, where of course a huge bounty awaits the retailer who can perfect the first system whose voice cannot be identified as that of a computer. Until that glorious day, when all call centres work with the efficiency of the Starship Enterprise's computer, we have to make a compromise. If your customers have a problem with IVR, it's that they are being asked to compromise too much.

Of course, what people hate about IVR isn't necessarily the technology itself. They just hate bad IVR. And it's the bad IVR that

me-t@iling

sticks in your mind. Whenever two or three cinema-goers are gathered together, one will eventually complain that it took them fifteen minutes to book a ticket over the phone while a trance-inducing voice said 'WWEELLCCOOMMEE tooo the Oooooodddeeoonnn Ccinneemmaa tiiicckkeeettt hhoottlliiiiinnnnee', a line that's about as hot as a cinema foyer in February.

Despite these setbacks though, surveys suggest that IVR is in danger of getting a good reputation – perhaps we're using it so much today that we've forgotten how often we do. Whether we are picking up voicemail, checking our bank balances or dialling our home answering machine, then we're using it daily. When the Henley Centre did a survey on behalf of BT, 45 per cent of consumers said they thought IVR improved service a little. Another 15 per cent thought it improved service a lot.

So what are the principles of good telephone-based self-service? To find out, we turn to one of the people who gave us the opportunity, (or cursed us with it, depending on your point of view), David Berger. He's been in the call-centre industry since it started in the UK, setting up some of the largest centres in the country, and now he's retired to tell other people how to do it through his consultancy, Callcentric. Berger readily admits to suffering from 'phone rage' in the last few years, because he's sick of being bounced around bad telephone systems.

Check your customer logs. If he's in there, he was probably the man bellowing impatiently at one of your agents this morning. "95 per cent of all call centres are a waste of time," he says. "All they do is annoy their customers. People don't think the process through." Berger has thought it through. These are some of his thoughts.

principle one: don't just do it to save money

Self-service for a call centre saves you money if you want it to. You can't argue with the sums. Figures for an American bank show that the cost of dealing with everyone in person at a call centre means that each transaction costs $1.27. When you allow users to serve themselves, it cost drops to 38c per transaction – less than a third of the cost, which is, of course, very tempting.

But if you pursue only cost-cutting as an objective, you'll eventually hit a brick wall. If you force everyone to go through IVR, those customers who don't want to use it will leave you. Then those who don't mind, but sometimes want to talk to a human, will follow. Fairly quickly, you will have trimmed your customer base, cut out all your excess margin and in the process driven out your most talented staff and perhaps your premium customers. You'll have no strategy for attracting new ones.

"Consolidation is totally the wrong reason to put in a call centre. You should be doing it to grow your business, not save costs. There's a cash-in-pocket benefit, but you're driving down your business," Berger says. "A lot of huge companies will disappear over the next few years because they can't grasp this."

Is this a familiar state of affairs? For many companies, the cash saving is top of the list when they are driving to introduce self-service technology at the call centre. What's slipped down the list is the difficult job of using telephone-based self-service to improve your basic customer service. How do we do this?

principle two: give your customers a choice

Remember at the beginning of the book, more than half of United Airlines ticket purchasers in the USA thought that buying tickets using a voice recognition system was just swell? At that point, you probably thought, 'What about the other half who hate it?' Luckily, so did the airline.

Giving customers the choice whether or not they want to serve themselves is a fundamental part of IVR. If they don't want to, then you're letting them down by telling them that the only option is to talk to a machine. You might be more prepared to help the customers who make you money, compared to the customers who aren't making much of a profit for your business, but as long as you apply your information to provide the personal service where it makes most profit for your business, this is not a crime.

On the other hand, telling your customers that this is the only way they can be served is a glorious way to turn certain customers away. Which ones? They might be difficult customers who endlessly clog up your call centre with outrageous requests, in which case you are happy to lose them. Or they might be your top 10 percent who know how profitable their business is for you and know they can get good service elsewhere. You don't really want to lose them.

And if you are giving customers a choice, do it early. Don't wait for them to exhaust themselves in your IVR system before you let them talk to a human. It should be common sense. But to be that, it would have to be common, and on the evidence we have, it isn't.

principle three: make it easy to do business

"A call centre," says Berger, "is a place where you get through to one person and that person can do everything for you that you want done." This still applies, even if that person is an automated message. Service has to be complete and easy to find.

Retailers put the best-selling lines at eye level, so why don't IVR systems do the same? Put the most common request at the start of a list and not only do you keep more customers happy, but you shorten the time they are on the phone to you. Bury important items at the bottom of a the third menu, which then forces the customer to call another number, and you're making them feel like a nuisance for wanting to help themselves.

principle four: make it quick to do business

This is convenience shopping. If it takes three times as long in the

IVR system as it would to phone up and ask a real person, then your customers will twig this. And if you nevertheless force them back into the IVR system, they will twig something else about your attitude to them, perhaps something you don't really want them to think. Self-service, whether in person, on the telephone or on the Internet, is a way to beat queues, not a new way to wait.

principle five: try it out

If you have a call centre and you're in a position to improve it, how often do you call it? Plenty of managers listen in at the agent's shoulder, but become a secret shopper and you'll understand what makes Berger so mad. "I'd love to record a number of calls to companies, send it to the chairman and say, 'This is how you represent yourselves to your customers'. There's no use blaming the software." And if you can't get it right, what does he suggest? "Pack up, go home and don't embarrass your customers."

The good news is that IVR can be very good indeed, when it's properly used. Take some of the work done by Speechworks with retail stockbrokers, including E*Trade and Charles Schwab. Here is an industry where serving your customer on time isn't just important, it's essential. The growth of retail investors on both sides of the Atlantic has made this frankly impossible to do: margins are tight (if you are making £15 a trade as your gross margin, you don't want to give each customer too much attention). That's why this is a natural for self-service. Customers know what they want to buy and how much they want to pay for it. There's no delivery problem if you're buying a thousand Marks & Spencer shares. They don't come in different colours or thicknesses.

The retail brokers figured out that this could fit well on the Internet and have been gloriously successful at doing it, as we have seen. But their customers are not always near a PC with a secure Internet connection and enough privacy to make a trade. Millions of trades every year are performed by telephone and not just trades either – thousands of customers every day call their broker simply to find a price.

me-t@iling

The result is that customers are being forced to wait by retail stockbrokers for up to thirty minutes during busy periods. And, of course, busy periods in any retail environment are exactly when customers want to do business. But it's also impossible for a stockbroker to predict with any accuracy when there's going to be peak demand.

The problem has reached such a scale that some frustrated investors are suing their stockbrokers because of trades that they missed. This is not customer service, and there's no way to solve the problem in the traditional call-centre environment.

Traditionally, you staffed a call centre for 95 per cent of peak demand. Lose one or two calls at that time, and it is acceptable. The cost of overstaffing at other times does not seriously affect your business competitiveness. When, however, the peaks and troughs are extreme and unpredictable, this model does not work. Staffing at 95 per cent of peak demand is too expensive, but staffing at less than 95 per cent makes waiting interminable.

Not all retailers are in a business as volatile as the stock market. But, in the future, retail peaks and troughs may become harder to predict as the times that we choose to shop on the telephone become more varied – or coincide with periods when call centres are dealing with international business.

Speechworks offers a self-service solution: it uses simple speech recognition to let stockbroker customers serve themselves without having to go through an IVR nightmare. Imagine that a virus which deletes all your files is found in the latest version of Windows (this isn't true by the way). News breaks worldwide and immediately you want to sell your Microsoft stock, as do thousands of others. You can wait for half an hour to say "What's the price on Microsoft?" to an agent, by which time it is half the price it was when you dialled, or you can use IVR.

Tone recognition is not practical here. If you have a list of companies, how do you select them? Press one for Asda, two for Ford, three for General Electric, four for IBM – and so on. This might take longer than holding in the queue!

Instead, Speechworks has designed a system that recognizes which company name you say. It doesn't have to recognize every word in the language, as if you were dictating to it, because there are only going to be a limited number of words you will say at any time. So, in our example, it recognizes a limited number of company names, asks you if it has guessed right, and recognizes 'yes' or 'no' in reply. The result is a cut in waiting times from half an hour at peak times to no time at all.

IVR is suited for simple, repetitive tasks, but sometimes it is surprising how many of the tasks your business performs are simple and repetitive.

The benefits? You save money, customers save time. But there's also a side benefit – those call-centre agents who are accustomed to dealing with angry customers are freed to talk only to customers who want more from the service. It's a motivating factor for retail customers, but it is also a motivator for the huge slice of the population who are call-centre agents.

internet

If 'call centre' has become a phrase you don't mention in polite company, then 'World-Wide Web' has had a comparatively easy ride from public opinion. Whereas the call centre has been criticised for dehumanising customer service, the web, on which nobody knows you're a dog, has been treated as its saviour.

But, in reality, much customer service on the web is no better than anywhere else. It's just different and novel. Because of the Internet's focus on self-service (there's no way to make someone come to your site, and there's no way to directly influence them when they are there), it is also a massive demonstration of the advantages and pitfalls of self-service shopping.

The practical risks of web shopping for the retailer and consumer are dealt with later. They are real, they are important, and, if they don't derail this gravy train, they will at least apply the brakes. Whether privacy and security are respected or not, shopping on the Internet has to be a good experience. It has to be easier, quicker, cheaper or it has to offer access to goods that shopping off the net doesn't give us. Sometimes it is all four but surprisingly often, it's none of the above.

We have talked about self-service applications as machines that retailers build for a customer to use. The World-Wide Web is simply the largest self-service machine in the world. It's a machine that one in five adults and three in five businesses use in the UK. It's a machine that maybe 200 million consumers worldwide (give or take 100 million) know how to use. It's a machine that is almost as accessible to the over-fiftys, who are the fastest-growing population on the web, as to the under-eighteens.

For retailers who grasp the principles of selling on the web, this is an opportunity that has just fallen from the sky. Or rather, it has risen from the telephone cables. Compare this with the difficulty of changing consumer behaviour in supermarkets, where convincing people to use self-service devices is a significant problem. On the net, customers are dragging retailers into offering goods for sale. Demand is not the issue, satisfying that demand is.

The problem is that we're still learning how to integrate this radical self-service machine with the existing retail structure, to make them complementary – to make them work even. It doesn't help that while control of retail premises, or management of a call centre, has traditionally been a board-level, operational issue, running the web site has been under the control of the marketing department. Perhaps this is why two-thirds of large retailers are unable to reply to an e-mail within forty-eight hours, or why 85 per cent of web retailers can't organise shipping overseas for goods ordered from their site. Customers are knocking on the door only to find there's no one at home who can help.

There's no time to sort this out. Web shoppers are, in the jargon, empowered to shop elsewhere. When you are accustomed to helping yourself, it's as quick to help yourself from one web site as from another. It's a lot quicker, because if you can help yourself easily, you save many times the amount of time it took to switch sites. Loyalty is fragile on the web, so retailers who make mistakes today start to lose customers immediately.

Here's an example. Drug dealers in the UK are suffering unexpected competition – from Dutch dealers running web sites.

The principles of self-service on the web could fill three books by themselves. But it is a mistake to look at the web in isolation. The trick is to create a self-service operation on the web without disrupting an established retail business, so that it is an asset to it rather than a distraction from it.

But you can't run a sub-standard web operation and not expect it to detract from your existing business any more. If there is no other reason why you have to get self-service right, if you take nothing else from this book, believe this. If two out of five of your customers are already using the web, then two out of five are likely to come to you on the web, looking to service themselves with goods, information or just to have a good time. If you let them down, do you think they will not use that failure to judge the brand? Think again.

Ian Smith, Oracle's UK managing director and a former head of BT's customer service operations, explains it from his own experience: "Last week I filled in a form on the web, then I got the same form through the post to fill out in ink. That immediately says to me, 'there's no connection here between your Internet channel and your

me-t@iling

correspondence channel'. That makes me nervous – it's sending the signal that the Internet is a bolt-on."

"We're taking 6 million phone calls a year, have 3 million IVR messages, but then the Internet team was separate again," says Stephanie Rouse, who runs business development for call centres representing The National Blood Service, Marks & Spencer and the Passport Office. "When someone called us who had contacted us via a different route a few days previously, we had 'corporate amnesia'," she says. The left hand of the company had no idea what the right hand was doing.

This, as we have seen, is the problem with self-service. It strips away the intermediaries in customer service so the customer can see exactly what you do (and do not) know. It leaves no doubt as to what service you do (or do not) offer. There is no way to dodge this question, so if your correspondence channel does not link to your web channel, it's not an internal issue. Its main effect is to punish your users for trying to help themselves by making them fill in the same form twice. If your call-centre agents have no idea what the user was trying to find on the web the day before or has no record of the e-mail that user sent them, you're saying, 'When you are on the net, you don't matter to us'.

The second common problem with self-service on the web is a lack of guts. Perhaps the most apparently foolhardy idea in the history of self-service was the decision of computer-networking specialist Cisco Systems to make all its user complaints public by putting them on the web. It was an idea conceived in the panic when the support centre was being overwhelmed by users' reports of errors and problems with Cisco's useful, but very complex equipment.

The company reasoned that if users could go and look for the problem themselves among the logs of previous support calls, then perhaps not so many people would be stuck in a phone queue. Experts laughed at the idea. By publicising all the faults that users had reported, so the logic went, Cisco would lose more customers than it gained. By telling customers to sort it out themselves, the company was abdicating its responsibility to support them.

Today, Cisco claims that its self-service support saves the company $550 million every year. Compared to what it was in 1995, customer satisfaction is 20 per cent higher, and 77 per cent of customer questions are handled on-line. Only 2 per cent of fixes aren't correct.

This is radical customer service. The point is that by opening up a small, limited, self-service support operation – perhaps with a few 'approved' support questions – the company would have never achieved these savings, because users would have still called as a first option. It would have sent the message that the web and self-service as a route to customer satisfaction was not a serious option.

The third point to make is that the Lord, or Bill Gates, or someone, gave us this technology and we ought to use it.

One of the reasons why companies cannot answer their e-mail is because it is so hugely expensive to do so, for after adding staff costs, each e-mail can mean £5. When a web page generates several thousand e-mails a day, it can be the percentage decision to ignore the difficult ones.

Mike Wheatley, managing director of a company called Brightware, has a different solution. He sells software that guesses the meaning of an incoming e-mail and automatically composes an answer. Four out of five e-mails can be dealt with in this way, and only one in fifty replies doesn't answer the question correctly – which, don't forget, compares very favourably with what a hard-pressed call-centre typist can do. "A customer representative can only handle about forty e-mails a day. We can answer thirty a minute," says Wheatley.

What sort of company would do something so radical? Such risk-takers as Abbey National for one. Most prefer that their names are kept secret. "One customer asked us to build in a delay before the reply was sent so it seemed like a real person was handling it," says Wheatley.

The self-service channel that the Internet gives us is different in one obvious respect from the others — you can double or triple the amount of business you do overnight. Unless you have your own mechanisms to cope with this, self-service will quickly become no service at all. Throwing more people at the problem cannot be an answer, certainly not for ever. Having automated your 'front-office' for self-service, you're going to have to automate the 'back-office' too.

Another example is Tesco Direct's launch of its Internet shopping service when enthusiastic buyers were surprised to find that deliveries often included mistyping and mistakes in the order that hadn't been there when they sent it. That was because when the service started, orders came via e-mail to a call centre in Scotland. They were then retyped and faxed to the appropriate outlet to be fulfilled. Good for ten shoppers, not so good for ten million. Use the technology — as Tesco has now done — to make sure that, when an order goes in one end, it comes out the other end the same. That's what electronic mail guarantees.

There's plenty more to say about the call centre and the Internet's role in self-service. In the next chapter, we're going to look at a fundamental question that underpins the problems we've seen here. It's a simple question, but unless you've an answer, you can't make a success out of self-service.

CHAPTER 5
have we met?

The question is this: do you know who your customers are? If you don't, or don't attempt to know them, then self-service becomes a way to become semi-detached from that customer. You lose the ability to find out what they want from you. You lose the ability to give them more of what they want. You lose the ability to upsell – to stretch your relationship with them further – because there is no relationship to stretch.

In the self-service arena, one type of marketing really counts – one-to-one. The fact that 70 per cent of your customers like something, doesn't mean that I like it when I come to you. If you try and force it on me, then I, like three out of ten of your customers, will immediately get the message you send along with it – we don't know who you are, we're using self-service as a convenience. In the 1990s, a technology called data warehousing became the vogue as a way of profiling customers. While it most certainly has advantages and can achieve great results, for many users it has been a failure. It is important to understand why.

the data warehouse
A 'data warehouse' is a giant database, or series of databases, which store everything there is to know about a customer, and from which you can analyse that customer's behaviour, likes and dislikes. Its purpose isn't to look at individual customers, but to make judgments about typical customer patterns. The best-known story, variously attributed to Wal-Mart, K-Mart and just-about-every-other-Mart, was the discovery that a large proportion of nappy purchases were accompanied by beer purchases, presumably because the husband,

having been sent out for nappies, would also pick up a six-pack for the fridge. So the nappies and the beer were moved closer together.

It's a good tale, whether or not it is true. At their best, data warehouses can tell us a great deal about typical customer segments. Where they come unstuck is when retailers try to model individual behaviour, or to recommend a course of action, as a result. You can't use a conventional data warehouse to produce a segment of one person. It's like trying to slice a grape with a chainsaw. This is because a data warehouse is very vulnerable if it receives poor data. For example, you do your weekly shop at a supermarket which is relatively cheap. When you want to buy food for a dinner party, you shop at a more expensive supermarket at which the food is of higher quality and tastes better. To the data warehouse at the first store, you are a cut-price bargain shopper. To the staff at the other shop, you are a premium, high-margin shopper. Both would choose to market to you based on those assumptions. Both would be wrong and missing a big opportunity.

Here is another example. You have three bank accounts with the same bank (as I do) which were all were started at different times, for different reasons, at different branches, so the bank has no idea that they are all held by the same person (even though I keep telling it so). Then, even though one bank account has a balance of several thousand pounds, the bank's data warehouse tells you that you cannot have a cheque card for the other account, because the balance is too low to justify it. So the trick to knowing who your customers are is achieved by a data warehouse in the big picture – but in the small picture, it is all about personalization: knowing who the customer is when he or she approaches you, and being able to see immediately what that customer has done, bought or asked for before.

dot-comers

Unfortunately, this brings to mind the joke: 'If you want to go there, I wouldn't start from here'. Most retailers have little idea who their customers are. It's one advantage that the Internet-only retailers have – from minute one they identify their customers. Some will even make those customers fill in a profile in order to 'register'. First let's look at the dot-coms in more detail to see what some of them have achieved. Then we can look at how the traditional business environment can try and emulate – or better – their level of customer service.

We start, as every piece about the dot-com generation starts, at bookshop Amazon.com. How does Amazon know its customers? Three years ago, it didn't. Given the challenge of using every piece of information provided by its customers, Amazon has been feeding on scraps for a long time and knows exactly how to do it. What Amazon now owns is information gathered by the short, yet meaningful interactions that the retailer has had with all its customers, probably including yourself.

It knows which books you have bought from Amazon in the past. It knows what books you are searching the site for, and it knows what customers who bought those books also bought. It knows what customers who bought the book you are looking for thought, because it has asked them to submit reviews. It knows what subjects you are interested in. For example, if you have bought several books on grooming your pet dachshund, this could be meaningful. It also knows your address, and, if that's how you have chosen to pay, it knows your credit-card number, billing address and expiry date.

So, in the short time that Amazon has access to you, it first of all responds to your requests in as efficient a way as possible by matching your search. It tailors its limited advertising to you as a customer, suggesting only products in which it calculates you have an interest at that moment, using the information from your search. It offers books that similar customers have ordered as suggestions. It tells you what other people in your community of bookbuyers thought of the book you are looking at. It lets you buy it without any fuss – indeed, if you're a returning customer, it lets you buy with one

me-t@iling

click of a mouse, because it has saved your credit-card details. You have twenty-four hours to cancel your order – a no-risk impulse buy.

The next stage for Amazon, and a work in progress for the year 2000, is to integrate its other businesses to upsell successfully to a self-service shopper. Amazon also sells pet food, via its sister company, Pets.com. So if you're a dachshund book purchaser, you might be happy to buy dog food too, if it was suggested at the right moment. Amazon has decided that every single mouse click is useful – and has to a large extent been proved right. So you get a personalized shopping experience using some element of data warehousing – suggesting books that 'similar' customers have bought. But its service depends more on analyzing what you are doing at that moment, and what you, as a customer, have done in the past. In some way, every single interaction is meaningful.

If you can collect that data, self-service doesn't mean that the customer becomes anonymous. It means exactly the opposite: self-service becomes a far more intensely personal shopping experience than we have ever known. For the first time our 'shop assistant' knows what we need before we have to tell it. Knowing the customer doesn't necessarily mean forcing information out under duress – the approach of 'fill in a form for me' is increasingly being outmoded on the net. Instead, the idea of 'community', where a site puts users in touch with like-minded people and encourages those people to ask for what they want, is becoming the norm. The former chief executive of IPC Electric, Rene Carayol, whose job was to take IPC magazine readers (think *Woman's Own, NME* and *New Scientist* to name three) and turn them into visitors to web sites – and purchasers from those web sites – has a clear view about what makes self-service shoppers return.

"There are the three Cs of on-line retailing," he says, "'Content, Creativity and Community. Actually, the only one that matters is Community." Community matters, he says, because it makes the customer feel he or she belongs, and will want to come back. A lowest-common-denominator self-service experience, whether it is on site, over the telephone, on the Internet or by television, is flawed because it carries no incentive to return. There's nothing offered beyond the transaction. If all your self-service retailing does is save costs, then on the net you run the risk of a 'race to the bottom', where you, and the competition, successively squeeze out margins until you're left with no bottom line and few satisfied customers. So IPC Electric didn't just put its magazines on-line and offer some marketing around that. It attempted to create an area where users would encounter a set of people and values that they could sympathize with and products that reflected those values.

becoming part of a community

That's when self-service becomes something more profound: when it starts to become self-actualization. You're not selling a product, you're selling the opportunity to be part of something. Another example is when you join an Internet stockbroker and get the opportunity to buy and sell shares. But you also get investment advice, company data, share price analysis and analyst estimates. E*Trade knows that, if all it sells is the chance to trade, there will be no customer loyalty. Instead, it's offering the chance to become part of a 'share owners' club'. Part of that deal is the guarantee that if something is not right, or could be improved, the retailer will take care of it.

"Look at Yahoo or Amazon; those companies are adapting their customer relationships on a daily basis," says Ian Smith, Oracle's managing director, who is currently nagging his customers in traditional retail to do the same thing. "It's an attitude of mind to say that they are constantly monitoring how they communicate with customers. To do that, they have to tinker with their customer applications all the time. Tinkering with your application is OK." The argument is that in the world of self-service creating a community of known customers isn't a bonus. It's a prerequisite. Otherwise, your self-service application will be instantly vulnerable to competition. The first reason is that self-service squeezes out margin – whether

me-t@iling

it is on the net or the high street.

There's an argument that new retail models, from Direct Line Insurance onwards, do exactly that. Market-watcher Robin Bloor, CEO of Bloor Research, calls it the 'death of ignorance' among consumers. His argument is that if the competition is a telephone call, a TV channel or a mouse-click away, if your products are constantly being compared in public with the competition's products, and if you are telling the customers that they have the power of choice, then price-matching becomes a prerequisite. It gets you to the start of the race, but it can't win it for you. If this creates a class of consumers who are prepared to shop around (and you have to be very lazy not to shop around on the Internet for a start), then it is vital to give them a reason to return. By creating a community, you create the chance to gather knowledge and offer relevant rewards.

This is easier to do in some markets than in others. Amazon's business plan was written for this type of sales opportunity. BP's was not. What's the community at a garage? Well, imagine that the garage has captured which make of car you drive. The motor industry knows a great deal about what type of people drive what type of car – so why not offer self-service customers relevant products while they fill their cars with petrol? After all, they're already committed to spending money, they're probably tired, hungry, bored or late, and they have nothing to do for the next sixty seconds but stare at the petrol pump.

If the customer is using a loyalty card at the pump, then why not take the opportunity to use the stored information on that loyalty card to offer more personally targeted advertising or help? To do that requires the ability to identify the customer in real-time and offer relevant products simultaneously. It's a tough job, but one that most providers of computer solutions consider they can handle.

learning from the customer

This is a job that isn't just useful for self-service, it's a job that only self-service can do. There's no point in stopping people at a petrol pump to ask them what products they want to see advertised. Surprise them by knowing already. You need to get to the point where you have the sort of hold on customers that enables you to know, every time they approach the store, the pump or the machine, who you are dealing with. On the Internet, this is easy. Customers want to identify themselves and will happily fill out a form, enter their credit card details (provided you can assure them it is for a quicker, more secure check-out) and even give profiling information.

At Oracle, Smith sees this as another lesson traditional retailers can learn from the dot-coms. "Having been in customer service for the last thirty years, I know that we finally have the tools so that people can serve themselves," he says. "But everyone misses out on the fact that when you first do business, the customer will spend time educating you. I will happily spend fifteen or twenty minutes filling in details. And it's not 'how many children do you have?'. It's questions about my lifestyle that mean something."

His experience suggests that if you ask your customers to tell you how much they earn in a year they will choose not to tell you, but if you ask them what car they drive and what their house is like they'll be very happy to tell you. It's effectively the same information. In fact, the lifestyle information is more useful. The next step is to wait for them to come back (and Smith's reasoning is that, if they have spent that much time giving you information, they have to come back 'to get their money's worth'), then immediately show them some advantage that pays them back for offering the information. Demonstrate that they can pop in any time they want and you'll remember their details from day one. If you miss this opportunity, he says, then you have broken the thread that binds them to their community.

me-t@iling

loyalty

How do we replicate this off-line? The most obvious idea is the loyalty card and loyalty schemes in general in self-service retailing. While loyalty cards have proliferated – and schemes like Air Miles have become a massive source of customer data that crosses boundaries between retailers – the self-service environment is both an opportunity and a problem. The opportunity is that the card becomes the single key to identifying your customer. The problem is making customers work the self-service machine this way without alienating them. So, for you as a customer, if asked by the self-service device for your card, it could be for an immediate benefit – think of the Boots Advantage card kiosk as an example. Or, more prosaically, think of a vending machine in Blockbuster Video that needs the membership card before it dispenses the video and is, in effect, saying, 'this is for members only'.

When the card is the gatekeeper, every self-service transaction for that card is a single customer's transaction. And you know that every time your customer shops self-service you have a record of the transaction. That's the ideal, but it's not realistic in some environments. Imagine your customer forgets his or her loyalty card in your shop – are you going to turn that customer away? So in environments where membership isn't obligatory, you need some incentive to make sure the customers don't forget the card. When we talked about self-scanning, we discussed variable pricing – cheaper shopping for loyalty card holders. That's an advanced application (and you might think a potentially risky one if two shoppers side-by-side found they were paying different prices).

A simpler incentive might be to make one in every hundred baskets of shopping free for loyalty-card holders. Managing this loyalty card information is also fundamental. Your customers don't want self-service to be a way of isolating them from the benefits of a loyalty scheme – but that's a common fault. "To have long-term profitable relationships with customers you have to know who they are," says Cap Gemini's head of CRM, Caroline Mansley. "You could be lucky enough to have a well-established loyalty scheme, and to know what your customers are like. Not many companies have that. And those that do have the problem of integrating it with the other information that they have."

An example – how many retailers who are part of a loyalty scheme allow their customers to register their loyalty cards on their web site? And of those who do, how many offer loyalty incentives specifically for self-service shopping? Unless self-service embraces loyalty, it's not only the retailer that's losing information, but the customer who is being treated like a second-class person.

This is another field in which the dot-coms have it easy. Loyalty schemes on the net are easy to administer, because you know your customer as soon as he or she logs on to the site (before then, if you use a 'cookie' – a piece of data that you send to the customer's computer as an identifier). This gives ample opportunity to make simple loyalty gifts. After shopping at www.jungle.com last week, I was told at the checkout that I could pick two free gifts, because I was a regular customer (the site greets me automatically with 'welcome back Tim'). As the managing director of jungle.com, Steve Bennett says, "In this environment you only get two chances to touch the customer. Once when they buy, and once when you deliver."

A more ambitious web loyalty program is Beenz (www.beenz.com). Don't be put off by the silly name. This is deadly serious. The loyalty card is a blunt weapon for attracting customers – either they use it, or they don't. Once that customer is in your shop or your site, there's little you can do to influence their behaviour. 'Beenz' are units of loyalty of very small denomination, which can be selectively applied to web sites to guide the customer – small incentives for small amounts of loyalty. So, while you may earn 100 Beenz for buying some CDs, you can also get 50 Beenz for giving up personal information by registering. You could even earn the odd Been – which I believe should be the singular – for loading a single page or looking at a special offer.

me-t@iling

Beenz are centrally administered and licensed to member retailers to distribute how they choose – customers can eventually cash in their Beenz, like Green Shield stamps, for items from the retailers' stores. Retailers get to share customer data. As an idea, it's still in the 'interesting curiosity' stage, because, as yet, Beenz has still to attract the really big names in retailing, many of whom prefer to run their own loyalty programmes.

How can traditional retailers learn from the model used by Beenz? With a loyalty programme, it's a lot harder to influence customer behaviour than it is on the web. You can't offer loyalty points for browsing shelves. However, you can offer a simple system of bonuses (as many retailers already do). The next generation of self-scanning systems can already pick out these bonuses for shoppers and alert them when they are in the right aisle, showing the discount or the points benefit in a small LCD attached to the trolley. This is Star-Trek stuff for most retailers, but it's a future that could be a matter of months away. And, with the Internet, digital TV and telephone-based home shopping to compete against, this version of loyalty may be what it takes to know, and keep, your customers.

Loyalty incentives are half the story. Personalization, as we have seen at Amazon, is the other aspect of upselling. It's possible today to personalize your message for self-service shoppers by putting that 'personal touch' into the machine you use. In fact, that's the only way you will do it. Today's new generation of ATMs (and almost all of the 24,600 ATMs in the UK will have to be upgraded in the next few years to prepare us for the next generation of credit cards) can provide this service. It's not about recognizing the customer by a fingerprint, scanning a retina for identification or recognizing the user's facial expression to guess what mood he or she is in – though all of these are possible today. It's a lot simpler.

Consider the story of the ATM user who always takes out £50. For six months, he takes out £50 on every visit to the ATM and always gets a receipt. The ATM says, 'Please take your money' and 'Please take your advice slip'. After six months, the software is upgraded. The next time he visits the ATM, it says, 'Would you like your usual £50 Mr Phillips?' and automatically gives him a receipt when he says he would. If that customer was then offered a way to submit personal information – imagine a web site in which he could enter family birthdays, wedding anniversaries, reminders that the mortgage payment will be leaving the account in a week, even his own birthday ('Many happy returns Mr Phillips') – such information could be useful to both parties. For the fictitious Mr Phillips, there's the warm feeling that the bank knows something benign about his spending habits and wants to help. For the bank, there's additional knowledge about the customer.

The bank ATM is a specialized device which is well suited to offering this type of service in the future. Loyalty of a sort is built in – because, if you want money, there are few other places to get it. But, as a self-service device, it's not so different in function from a call centre. The modern call centre has to combine three routes to the customer – traditional phone service, the type of self-service IVR that we saw in the previous chapter and communication through the web.

If we're talking to a live agent, it's not unsual to hear ourselves being upsold. The information from the last call is there, it's ready to use and there's an accepted way to use it. But unless those upselling messages can reach out to self-service customers when it's appropriate, then two-thirds of the customer interaction is being lost. Unless the feedback from the self-service customer gets back to the telephone agent, then two-thirds of that customer is also being lost.

if you don't ask, you don't get

The central tenet of this personalization story is that if you don't ask, you don't get. But asking can take more than one form. In everyday life, we don't find out if our loved ones are happy or sad by saying "Are you unhappy today?" We listen to the story about the nightmare day at work, then make a pretty accurate guess. In meetings, we

me-t@iling

don't say, "Are you unhappy with the proposal?" We look at the pile of torn-up paper on the floor and make a guess. So it is with self-service. Your customer may explicitly offer information at the beginning. By acting intelligently on that information, the customer will offer more information. As we saw, answering e-mail automatically can be done with an astonishingly high accuracy. That e-mail gives valuable insights into the problems your users have and the new features that interest them. If you encourage them to send it, they'll respond.

An even more direct route to customer feedback is at www.one2one.co.uk, where Yasmin answers questions that you type into a box at the top of the screen. Yasmin doesn't exist, except as a few thousand lines of code, as is obvious. No one is trying to hide it. But if you have a question about your mobile phone service, the Yasmin program will try and understand the question, and give an answer. Compared with having to wait for a reply, or to wait in a phone queue or visit a shop, few users are going to mind that they didn't talk to someone. And more users are going to want to ask Yasmin more questions.

These questions are also valuable customer feedback. If your customers have identified themselves by logging on to the web site, that becomes extremely useful personalization information too. But only if you act on it. By making the process of information-gathering one which benefits the customer, you will inspire loyalty, which produces more information that you can use both at a macro level – by segmenting these customers – and at a micro level – by approaching each customer with a targeted message every time the customer does business with you.

To do this though, all the 'intelligence' has to be built into your machine – and be available to the customer at a time when it's useful. All the data you collect has to be integrated immediately. Customer information has a short half-life – the longer you keep it before you act on it, the poorer the information becomes. This process has reached its ultimate expression at The Popcorn Factory, a US-based sweet retailer ('Inside our 2 gallon Bunny Garden tin is butter, tangy cheddar and homemade caramel corn. For a really neat treat try our scrumptious chocolate drizzled caramel corn'). The factory isn't just waiting for customer data, it's generating it: every week, it experiments with new products, new ideas, new types of customer service – just to get a reaction. It prods its customers to see if they say 'ow'. Every day, it monitors that reaction. If it's a good reaction, it makes the change permanent. If it's bad, it scraps the idea.

As a self-service machine, this goes a step further – it is using its customers to create feedback, so that it becomes self-improving. Not all web retailers 'get it' – but the best ones do. Compared with the level of personalization they achieve working with customers that they will never meet, the efforts of many traditional retailers and the struggles of some call centers to provide 'personal service' may soon seem rather lame. Self-service doesn't hide the behaviour of individual customers. Provided you can identify these customers, it exposes it more clearly than ever – even compared with the days of 'personal service' in the much-lamented corner shop. Everything tomorrow's self-service customer does can be logged, analysed, acted upon to a retailer's advantage. Customers will continue to give up personal information – either knowingly or unknowingly – because you are paying them for it. Provided, of course, you let them know that you care.

CHAPTER 6
more bright ideas- help yourself

'Attention Kmart shoplifters: refunds! Unwanted stolen items can now be replaced prosecution-free,' says the headline. 'Arguing that there is no such thing as bad customer loyalty, Kmart yesterday unveiled a new shopper returns policy allowing defective or unwanted stolen items to be exchanged or returned for a full refund,' it continues. The article quotes Kmart chief executive Floyd Hall. 'Many shoplifters', said Hall, 'are young or low-income individuals who at some point may be able to pay for merchandise. When they can,' he said, 'We want them to think of Kmart'.

Don't panic, it's not for real. The retail industry hasn't gone completely mad. The piece is taken from a spoof newspaper called the *FNwire* (www.fnwire.com) which lives up to its catchphrase of 'Fast, Free, False'. As an application of self-service, it's no more surprising than some of the other schemes that are beginning to emerge. Some retailers will argue that it would be no less destructive to their business. But, if you believe that self-service ends with a web site and a scanner on your shopping trolley, you're fooling yourself.

So far we have treated self-service as if it's a new channel to market. Actually, this is only a small part of the story. It's a completely new market. If you're struggling to come to terms with the demands of adding a self-service channel to your existing sales operation, then here's the awful truth: this is just the beginning.

The next decade will see a revolution in the way we sell that will make the previous fifty years seem like a period of consolidation. And much of it is based around the idea that customers in the future will serve themselves. We have compared self-service to a machine to which you give the customer access. In the future, customers will build their own machines and give you access to them, or they will take your machine and change the way it is built, or they will tell you what type of machine they want and let you build it for them. Earlier we noted that once a self-service project is running, it's a basis for doing some really interesting things with the technology.

how it's going to work

In retailing, that means perhaps using variable pricing for loyal customers, or prompting users with recipe ideas. In mail-order, it can mean helping with comparison shopping or IVR. On the net, it can mean adding an assistant to offer advice automatically. There are many ways in which self-service will develop, but it is worth looking at a few of the most unusual ones, because they have one thing in common— they change the nature of retailing completely. They stand it on its head.

Look at it this way: retailing is a 'push' process. Sellers convince people to buy goods. The self-service economy is a 'pull' economy, where the same consumers decide that they want to come and buy things. It's only a matter of time before they begin to decide how they will buy things from you when they arrive, and how much they want to pay. If your business isn't ready for this wave of consumers, it's no big deal for them — because someone else will be, and they will be quite easy to find.

We're going to look at some of these new models, not to try and work out how successful they will be — not even they know that, although for many of these companies there are strong signs that they are here to stay — but to see what innovations they bring to self-service. There's an economic theory that the Internet reduces all transactions either to a pure market or an auction: either matching a price instantly becomes essential, or being able to respond by cutting your price is necessary. When you're competing with Internet retailers (and who isn't?), then that's going to be your market too.

me-t@iling

consumer power – letsbuyit.com

Letsbuyit.com is a 'buyers' club'. Talk to the company's CEO John Palmer and he's at pains to stress that his web site is not a retailer. It's an organizer. He employs one 'geek' and lots of retail buyers.

The process: the site suggests items that groups of consumers might want to buy – let's use last Christmas's example – Christmas trees. The buyers do a deal with the manufacturer, retailer, or, in the case of the trees, the importer. For 50 trees, say, the cost per unit would be at one level. For 100, or 200, or 500, the cost per unit falls. On the web site, buyers are then offered the chance to join in a group buy. When I bought my Christmas tree, the price was £11. A few days later, it had fallen to £7.

How far can self-service go? The customer is not so much king as omnipotent. I decided whether or not to buy. I decided at which price I would buy. I had a team of professional negotiators working for me, to ensure I got what I wanted. For retailers, it's the nightmare come true. If they refuse to deal with Letsbuyit.co.uk buyers, those buyers then go to the competition. If they agree to do a deal, they make less margin the more they sell. On the other hand, Letsbuyit is a device that circumvents traditional channels completely, renders them obsolete. It guarantees customers, so 'selling' becomes your ability to fulfill the order.

"Brits are being ripped off on the high street and we want to tackle that. Europe's retailing industry as a whole is inefficient, with lots of middlemen and a lot of margins being tacked on at every opportunity. We're trying to destroy the value chain as we know it and connect our members directly with manufacturers and distributors," says Palmer, in apocalyptic mood. It doesn't matter whether he's right or not. His ability to guarantee a discount (usually between 20 and 50 per cent) makes it look as if he's right! If there are weaknesses with Letsbuyit, they are concerned with how well this model can scale. It puts power in the hands of consumers who know what they want, but it's not a device for impulse purchases or if you want to browse. That's not holding Letsbuyit back though. It is already in fourteen countries one year after launch. In its first three months of trading, Letsbuyit picked up 50,000 users.

name your price – priceline.com

If as a retailer you thought that having consumers banding together to haggle with you is going too far, you might want to look away now. Through Priceline, your customers don't just tell you what they want, they tell you exactly how much they are prepared to pay for it. You'd be overstating the retailer's strength to call it 'haggling'. If you're a Priceline customer, you either go to the web site or call the freephone number and describe what you want. Imagine it's a hotel room in Chicago, and you don't want to pay more than $60, but you want at least three-star accommodation. Priceline's systems immediately relay the request to hotels who decide whether they want to take that business. If anyone accepts, then the reservation is made on the spot.

"Sellers participate because they always have more than they can sell, and Priceline customers are guaranteed buyers", the company says. So far this has worked for 2 million customers in the USA alone on hotel rooms and airline tickets and the company proudly claims to find customers for 30,000 flights a day, a substantial chunk of the 500,000 spare seats that US airlines have. Priceline hasn't started to compete in the UK yet, but it is broadening the range of goods it supplies. Spare hotel rooms are a natural for this type of sale, and late deals on flights are nothing new. Now, the company is offering to do you a deal on rental cars, on the purchase prices of new cars – 'Imagine buying or leasing the new car or truck of your dreams at the price you want to pay without ever having to haggle with a salesman' says the company – and even on groceries.

For the future – look out for the Priceline Gasoline card, so you can pay what you want for petrol.

me-t@iling

Priceline isn't an irrelevant, short-term phenomenon. It's already big enough in the USA to be a significant brand in its own right. It presents its business model as a win for both sides – the customer gets a bargain, the retailer gets rid of excess inventory – but it is only a matter of time before Priceline-type business begins to devour the existing, full-price business of the companies involved. But when the customers come calling, what do you do? Turn them away?

the race to the bottom – mondus.com

Auctions are often good for sellers, bad for buyers – playing off two potential customers against each other is a huge advantage. How you'll wish no one thought of the reverse auction, where one buyer plays multiple retailers against each other. This isn't anything new. In other words, it is 'shopping around'. The new retail model though, gives the process a formalism and transparency that it hasn't had before.

One of the most significant entrants in this market is Mondus.com which is built to work in favour of small business customers. You want to buy a computer? Put a tender out on Mondus for the computer you want, and retailers who will sell through Mondus can tender for the business. As the customer, you can pick the tender that works best: it could be the cheapest, it could just be the one that looks the most attractive. It certainly won't be the most expensive, and it probably won't be the first one that comes in. Mondus isn't just for buying computers: it's for stationery, electronics, even temporary staff. There is no negotiation with the customer. It's a machine that works on their behalf to squeeze out your margin.

business to business – Sears and Carrefour

We've treated self-service exclusively as if it's a business-to-consumer proposition (or for Mondus, a business-to-small-business proposition). But there's no reason why it should be. As with electronic commerce, the 'B2B' side may be much bigger, though possibly less glamorous. Try telling Sears Roebuck chief executive Arthur Martinez that. He calls GlobalNetXchange, his joint venture with

Carrefour and Oracle, 'a revolution in retail'. We're accustomed to the latest retail revolution being the most important occasion since, well, the last retail revolution before it. But just as Mondus.com has created an on-line market for businesses who want to sell to consumers, so GlobalNetXchange has a similar function for businesses that want to source the best-price product from suppliers. In this case, those businesses are Sears and Carrefour, and the site allows it to tender for suppliers in a 'reverse auction'.

So Sears wants a range of saucepans. The suppliers who can provide that range can put in a bid. An auction takes place – Sears picks the lowest suitable bid. It's self-service retailing, but instead of a relatively powerless consumer at the buying end, there's a multinational retailer flexing its muscles and achieving dramatic cost savings. Between the two companies, there's purchasing power of $80 billion a year from 50,000 suppliers. Suddenly, the traditional approach – a fixed-price, fixed-term contract with a named supplier – is outmoded. If you're a supplier for Carrefour or Sears, you suddenly have to deal with one of the wealthiest, most aggressive self-service customers of all. If you're a rival retailer, you're probably thinking, 'why didn't we think of that?'

Three other companies that did think of it are General Motors, Ford and Daimler Chrysler. They have also launched a similar service, allowing them to pick their suppliers after an auction. After decades of trying to shorten the supply chain or squeeze cost out of it by increasing efficiency, there's a new approach – why squeeze cost out of the edges when there's a big margin right in the middle of the business that the companies can attack? The web site is the mechanism, the self-service machine that eats away margin until the lowest-price supplier gets the job.

check it yourself – FedEx and UPS

We've mentioned this before, but it's worth looking at in more detail. Federal Express knows that a customer call to check on a parcel costs $2 to process. It also knows that a customer enquiry to its web

me-t@iling

site will cost 10 cents to process. Guess which method it prefers you to use? That's why it likes its customers to go to the web, type in their consignment number and check their own parcels – because the web site tells you exactly where it is. Having built this mechanism, Fedex decided that it was of limited usefulness just covering its own shipments for it could also cover the shipments that it makes on behalf of other retailers. The same goes for rival UPS, which offers a similar service. Go to many of the on-line shops on the web today, and parcel tracking is standard, not because their systems can track the shipment, but because they have outsourced their shipping.

I spoke to a small Internet retailer called El Celler Catala. Actually, it's one person on a farm outside Barcelona selling wine called Peter Hodder-Williams. If you want to know where your case of Cava has gone, just check with his site – your order details are there for you to see. But it's not Hodder-Williams who is providing them. It's UPS which tracks the packages from when they leave his farmhouse to when they arrive at your door. The service comes as part of the deal with his on-line shop, which is leased to him by Yahoo!, and hosted by them. 'It's not terribly complicated,' he admits – his idea of refreshing the retail environment is a few hours a week updating his web page. The result is that small businesses who don't have the time, the skill or the technical expertise to build their own self-service customer service model can plug into those that already exist.

price comparisons – www.shopgenie.co.uk

Much of the 'new retail' is dedicated to helping achieve lower prices by bartering or auctioning. The price-comparison model is different. It's a simple device that lets shoppers pick the cheapest price. So far there aren't many of them, and they don't do much, but they are guaranteed to become a part of the retail landscape in the next few years. Go to the site, tell it what book, CD, computer game or other commodity you are looking for and ask it to search for you. The comparison-shopping site sends out a 'bot' (as in robot), a software program that looks in every web retailer it can find for the right price. Then it offers you the list of prices it finds, with availability, and with postage and packing charges and VAT. As a customer, it's so pleasant to have someone to shop around for you. As a retailer, the potential pitfalls are many indeed.

The first is that a comparison-shopping site eats loyalty. In a previous chapter, we talked about the value of personalization as a way of keeping your customers bound into a 'community'. If retailers don't achieve enough personalization and the community isn't strong enough at the retail site, then customers will shift their community allegiance to a comparison-shopping site and use the retailers only when they are cheapest. In effect, the retailer has become a wholesaler. The other problem is that you can't stop it, even if you want to.

In the early days of comparison shopping, traditional retailers who found their Internet pricing being probed wrote their own software to keep out the 'bots'. This isn't hard to do, but what does it say about your business? 'We are afraid to have our prices compared'. That opacity can't survive the self-service economy. All that happens is that a customer who might have chosen your goods will certainly not choose them, because you have not made them available at the point of sale – the comparison shopping site. Instant response has always been an asset in retail (and outside it too). The ability to complete the sales cycle inside a single customer contact is vital in self-service – because there's no guarantee that a customer will ever come back. Offering a two-stage process is offering the customer a chance to disengage that might not serve anyone's interest.

Promise

Promise, the mortgage service set up by Credit Suisse in 1999, is one example of how effective targets for the level of service that an on-line presence can bring can lead to new ways of doing business. The service is designed to give users an instant quote, an instant decision and a full service afterwards. Anyone who has ever bought a mortgage will appreciate how many agencies this is likely to involve. In the first instance, this would be impossible without the ability to combine the front office (the mortgage offer and customer-facing

me-t@iling

technology) with the back office (the credit checking and validation that is an essential part of managing Promise's risk). At the site (www.ipromise.co.uk), users have the chance to get an instant quote.

The process has been simplified so that users can get the quote having answered five questions in a target time of four minutes. Users who want a mortgage can then fill in a form with a target time of twelve minutes. Running in the background while the customer is completing the form is an on-line credit check. The offer is then instantly made or declined, based on that process only. Getting a mortgage takes forty different activities, according to Promise, from surveys to conveyancing – the application that manages your mortgage offer triggers these forty activities automatically to guarantee completion in twenty-one days. The company hasn't tried to set a level of service and then automate parts of its operation to fit. It has designed the process from the beginning to be simple enough for a self-service customer, because, without that process, there would be few customers who have the confidence to use it. On the other hand, once a process has been defined, it raises the standard for traditional mortgage lenders. So far, no one else has been tempted to compete at this level of automation.

new channels – open

We've so far successfully ignored a spectacularly successful self-service channel, digital television. Already, almost as many houses have a digibox as have an Internet connection. Users who want to shop there can do so for free (provided, at the moment, that they use Sky Digital) through the shopping channel called Open. Open is what the industry likes to call 'lean-back' technology, rather than the 'lean-forward' technology of the computer. But it's two flavours of the same shopping experience: interactive content, digital payment, self-service methodologies.

So far, retailers like Somerfield, Next and WH Smith have set up simple interactive sites on Open to test the response – and early indicators are that it is overwhelming. Whereas surfing the net to shop is an alien activity that users have to trust to produce a good shopping environment, shopping on the television could offer more comfort. For retailers too it's a more comfortable self-service situation. Superficially similar to the web, it's in fact closer to the call centre with pictures. There's no opportunity for users to comparison-shop (Open controls who has access to its site) and there are no inconvenient buyers' clubs or reverse auctions to fear. Pricing is fixed, purchasing is instant.

There are great opportunities to be gained from interactive TV – not least that you have a channel to market your products to self-service customers by potentially building interactive advertising. While your potential customers are watching television, they can be given the chance to click on a button and go straight to the screen to buy the product that's being advertised. So far this has been trialled, but not put into practice. It's the kind of instant-response mechanism that could be a powerful tool for influencing your customers, and a tool that's not available on the phone and is not controllable on the net, where advertising banners are the nearest equivalent. Ultimately, the boundaries between entertainment and advertising could be broken down further, if the authorities allow it.

The technology which allows fake advertising hoardings and logos to be painted over a sporting event could also be used to deliver segmented advertising messages to customers who can choose to buy instantly. It's a possible future, not necessarily one that everyone will like, but one that only digital television can deliver, if that's what consumers demand. Digital television is a unique retail environment though. It's far more passive than other interactive technology, because when you are watching television, even interactive television, research suggests that you don't like doing very much.

Bruce Lynn, manager for Microsoft's UK web TV (a rival platform to Open that the cable companies will use) has been testing how to design a successful shop on TV. "Television is a simple device," he says, "Computers are complex. Good web design says that if you have twelve items on a menu, cut it to six. In the TV world, if you have six, cut it to three." Even that may be too many, he adds, because asking shoppers to make a decision can put them off. "Take a lesson from direct mail," he says. "The correct number of options to give someone is one." Of course, to give someone a single option, you have to know what that single option is. Digital television promises great returns for a mass-market customer. But unless you can successfully target that customer, retailers will either confuse them or leave them cold.

The other potential risk from self-service television is what it does to the broadcasters and by extension, its effect on the value of advertising. Digital television has alerted its viewers to the potential of pay-as-you-go television, not just for films and prize fights, but for soaps and news as well. A survey commissioned by NOP shows that 57 per cent of television watchers would prefer to pay for television using this method, rather than a flat-rate subscription every month as at present. If the broadcasters decide to resist this trend, then the shape of broadcasting, with scheduled packages bookended by advertising will persist. If scheduled television begins to break down, then so does the advertising model that goes with it. Customers will be much more able to 'screen out' unwanted messages. They might even demand a system that doesn't offer advertising for products they don't like.

Compare this to the music business, where the search for downloadable music has eclipsed the search for pornography as the most popular occupation for search engines, and we begin to see a trend. In the music business, the record companies cried foul, because they want to sell entire CDs, not one song at a time. But the lesson is that empowering the consumer means that services will become unbundled, packages will become separated into their constituent parts. The search for value will not end when the retailers say it ends. It will end when customers are happy that value is what they are getting. Interactive TV might be the clearest demonstration yet that retailers can't have self-service 'their way'.

buying on the phone – WAP and m-commerce

WAP, or the 'wireless application protocol,' to give it its full name, is an Internet derivative that sends Internet-like content to your mobile phone. Already the first WAP phones are on sale, and the first WAP services are on-line through the servers run by mobile phone network providers. If you want news, train times and stock prices in future, you can bring them up on the tiny screen of your WAP-enabled mobile phone. By the time you read this, half the population will have a mobile, and, by 2005, 70 per cent of our handsets will be WAP-enabled. Already companies like Woolwich and Halifax plan to offer WAP-phone banking, and shoppers will be buying from retailers using what, in the jargon that we love to use, has been christened 'm (for mobile)-commerce'.

At British Telecom, its group director Andy Green has a league table for how we will get our interactive content in future: "Mobile phones, TV sets, games machines and then the PC will be the way to access the Internet," he says. The advantage of WAP is that your self-service customer is easily in touch and always available to buy. But there's little chance for retailers to sell to them – even the best WAP phones have small screens and little chance for anything approaching conventional marketing. What they do offer is the chance to identify and personalize the service for a single customer. On the Internet nobody knows you're a dog, but, when you are using your WAP phone, anyone communicating with you knows exactly who you are. If the Internet implies that personalization is useful, then WAP makes it essential – because you don't have the time or the bandwidth to deliver the wrong message to your customer.

All these new ideas and new routes to market have benefits and risks. In the next chapter we'll look at some of the financial risks to both consumer and retailers in more detail, because it's the one area that could leave today's self-service crocked. But however closely you manage financial risk, there's plenty of evidence here that the business risk from radically new self-service ideas is just as real and could in the future be just as damaging.

CHAPTER 7
DANGER card not present!

In June 1997, police raided a suburban home in Dublin. Inside the house they discovered a secret hoard of stolen goods acquired by deception and credit-card fraud. With the stolen goods valued at a retail price of $2,000, this was no opportunist crook or petty thief.

Indeed it wasn't. The culprit turned out to be a fifteen-year-old boy, who had ordered the goods over the Internet, entering a random card number to pay for them. How did he get the number? Certainly not from anyone he knew, because the card-owner lives in Argentina. (He claimed he made the number up, which is possible but doubtful.) When the card-owner saw the charge on the bill, he alerted the authorities. The police described our apprentice crook as 'remorseful'. His hoard? Two grand's worth of Toffee Crisp, Dairy Milk and Mars Bars, hidden under his bed. "He's sick of the sight of chocolate," said a police spokesman, who added that our criminal mastermind was discovered "trying to consume the evidence".

Upstanding citizens John and Imogen Crichlow spent £700 on American pornographic web sites in 1999 – which was news to them when they got their credit-card bill. They first noticed the problem in March and alerted John's credit-card issuer, Lloyds TSB. "The manager at our local branch in Heathfield said they couldn't do anything until we had traced the origins of the transaction because, he said, in most cases customers have made the transactions but forgotten them. In disbelief – we had never bought anything over the Internet and had not lost our Visa cards – we had to phone a string of numbers in the USA that proved to be agencies for pornographic web sites."

The Crichlow cash had been spent by persons unknown with companies known as 'brown-wrapper' web sites, who disguise their identities on credit-card bills, presumably to avoid embarrassing genuine customers. For the Crichlows, it was an education – but not one they wanted.

The Crichlows gave the details to their bank to verify. Verification took two months. The details were passed on to Lloyds TSB Visa card services for investigation. That took three months. 'We do not know how their accounts were accessed,' said the apologetic bank, refunding the money, plus £25 for the wait. 'We do not want to scare people because it is extremely rare for this to happen.'

It's not that rare though. Credit card-fraud, after several years on the wane, is rising again, and the self-service retail business is the avenue through which this is happening. While the Internet is the most visible route for the credit-card fraudster, in truth, it is only the highest-profile example of card-not-present (CNP) fraud in the UK.

increasing problem

But it's certainly a significant problem. As we saw earlier, Visa International says that 2 per cent of its credit-card business relates to Internet transactions, but 50 per cent of its disputes and frauds relate to the Internet. 'This has become a significant issue for our industry,' said a company spokesman. 'It's all down to the problem of authentication, which has become the most important issue in our industry. Customers worry too much about fraud on the Internet, and merchants don't worry enough. Some merchants have told us they have had to triple the size of their dispute departments.'

The problems with fraud affect all of us. Consumers are scared of electronic commerce or finding unexplained charges on their cards, charges that customers who aren't as diligent as the Crichlows will never recover, or perhaps even notice.

Merchants may suffer fines and chargebacks from credit-card

issuers or the card associations — we'll cover this in more detail later. They may even have their ability to accept credit card-payments taken away. In the self-service arena, that means losing your supply of oxygen.

Acquiring banks, who do the processing of these transactions on behalf of their merchants, may face a rash of failed retailers — these losses become their losses. When thousands of credit-card payments are being queried, the cost of their overheads climbs — costs that may eventually be passed on to the merchant.

Credit-card issuers suffer a loss of customer confidence, a rise in their administration costs, and the potential defection of customers who blame them for the merchant's lack of security. If you want to see how big the fraud problem could get in the UK, look to the USA. It is, after all, a year ahead in terms of electronic commerce, so it's not exactly encouraging to see research by a consultancy called Meridien which has calculated that up to 15 per cent of all sales made over the net are fraudulent. In 2001, this means that US retailers will face fraud totalling $9 billion, which makes last year's $400 million loss seem quite modest by comparison. By 2003, the total will have ballooned to $15 billion — unless something is done to stop it. That would be $30 for every credit card in the USA, or around 3 per cent of the total credit card-spend, on or off the net.

In the UK, the credit-card industry body, the Association for Payment Clearing Services (APACS) admits that, between 1998 and 1999, CNP fraud increased 104 per cent to more than £20 million. That's 10 per cent of the total loss to fraud. While fraud in other sectors is at least under control, CNP has become a major worry to the credit card-industry, not least because the number of avenues for fraud is increasing every day. Those avenues are concentrated around commerce over the telephone and self-service, especially the Internet.

secure payment

We have talked in the previous chapters about self-service systems being designed to store and use customer data in real-time, and how desirable this is for a reseller looking to upsell or to cross-sell. Desirable it may be, and the business risk is considerable. If, however, the financial systems that back a self-service operation are not built just as robustly and are not able to authenticate credit cards in real-time, then these losses will continue to spiral. You can have the best customer data, the most carefully-planned retail offering, the easiest-to-use self-service device and the ultimate in personalization, but unless you can back that with a secure, robust payment system, fraud will find you.

In the self-service arena, fraud will find you quickly, and it will migrate to your application. Running a self-service business which has a reputation for being a soft touch is no better than running a store with no security staff. Once the word gets round – and on the Internet, for example, word can get right round the world in minutes – you're flooded with customers who want to help themselves. But it wasn't the help-themselves deal that you were hoping for.

In self-service, almost all transactions will be CNP transactions. On the net, every payment will be a CNP payment: around 99 per cent of the business-to-consumer payments on the net are made, and will continue to be made, by credit card. The problem with your CNP payments is that for retailers, the liability for fraud rests with them. It's outside the 'normal rules' of your credit-card transactions. When the fraudsters come calling from anywhere in the world, you pay the bill. How do we cope with this?

The first option is to abandon any self-service project or ambition, to throw away the proposal and pretend to the board that it wasn't your idea – something which seems very attractive about now. It's undoubtedly the route that some retailers will take. If the exposure risk of not adapting your business for the Internet, of not building a self-service offering through traditional channels is hard to quantify, this risk has scary numbers attached to it, and those numbers come straight off the bottom line.

me-t@iling

As we have seen, this may still be a false economy: the penalties for burying your head in the sand are severe. For example, of the top ten media companies on the web in the USA, nine are new, according to Morgan Stanley Dean Witter. That means a media company that decided to wait until there was a secure revenue stream from the net (almost all the traditional ones took this route) has been punished for it. In the USA, Bank of America paid $80 million in shares for 5 per cent of the on-line mortgage lender, E-loan, because it didn't want to take the risk of launching its own service, and discovered too late that the risk could be managed – an expensive failure of nerve.

managing the risk

Because so much of self-service retail is geared to instant gratification – you don't want to ask the customer to 'come back later' – the risk cannot be managed by employing more people behind the scenes. It has to be automated, it has to be instant. Few sales decisions in the self-service sector can be referred upwards. If you are referring a decision upwards, perhaps you need to redesign your fraud-management systems, because you're letting it get in the way of the sales process.

Ultimately the fraud risk in self-service applications can be managed, if not completely eliminated. There are technological solutions that can be brought to bear. There are companies and initiatives that will help: we're going to look at some of the work that one, Retail Decisions, is doing across the spectrum of self-service retailing. For retailers, fraud prevention is not an unknown discipline. The main problem is still to integrate these solutions sufficiently with your architecture.

Also, this is an aspect of self-service that can't be developed *ad hoc*. This isn't an area in which you can try a solution to see if it works, because, if it doesn't, it's inevitably an expensive mistake. It takes planning and strategic thought that needs to be conducted entirely separately from the whirlwind of developing the creative content, and that cannot be compromised for that content.

Integrating a team to make self-service happen is a prerequisite of business that we have spoken about in the past – the team has to contain elements of marketing, operations, sales, customer service – and it has to contain both representatives of your finance function and the right level of IT planning to ensure the self-service machines you build are not cash dispensers for the criminal fraternity.

There's one final general point to make. Self-service removes embarrassment for the shy, for people who want to make personal requests, for people who feel awkward talking to a live agent about money, and for people who just fancy a go at ripping you off. Many people who would not consider trying to hoodwink a live agent won't think twice about trying a fraud on your self-service machine. For them, it may be no more wrong than the traditional practice of thumping a vending machine to see if it gives you a free can of drink, (a self-service fraud issue that we regret we're unable to address in this book).

Before we get to the practical application of fraud-prevention methods, a word about the general risk of a poorly designed architecture in the self-service arena. If the machine you build isn't working properly, then honest customers and fraudulent ones alike will not be able to deal with you, no matter how much they want to. Even the 'blue-chip' e-commerce sites, sites like Ebay and Amazon, have suffered extended periods of unplanned downtime in the past year.

The cost of that downtime, lost revenue, lost opportunity, lost branding is like hanging a sign on your shop saying, 'we're closed, we don't know when we are going to be open'. Does that inspire confidence in your customers? Perhaps not, thinks Rene Carayol, ex-head of IPC Electric.

There are many ways in which downtime can be eliminated, too many to discuss here. But what's essential is that the application is divided into 'layers'. Just as a retail enterprise divides the tills from the racks,

me-t@iling

and divides the racks from the stock, so a self-service organisation has three distinct parts. At the bottom, the data on actual and prospective customers should sit in its own repository, engineered to be available twenty-four hours a day. This guarantees that your shop is available as much of the time as possible — and to multiple applications, for example, your call centre and your web site. When this information includes customer credit information, that availability is crucial to managing risk.

On top of that, the application that uses the data forms a separate layer. This is the 'self-service machine' that we've been talking about, but it also contains the business rules. This applies your risk management policy, no matter what the customer data is. It also means that your anti-fraud protection is bound into the application, not painted on the top like a moustache. At this layer, the application has to be as scalable as possible, so that if your business doubles, then processes like authentication can still run in a practical length of time.

The third layer is the interface with the customer. Keep this separate and you ensure that the same fraud-prevention rules apply whether the customers are communicating over the phone, in person or on the Internet. It avoids your business having susceptibility, a 'weak link' in the chain that can be exploited by cunning fraudsters.

This architecture itself doesn't manage fraud. It merely shows you a way to manage the process by which you manage fraud. There are, however, many other steps that you can take at a tactical level to make fraud management not just possible, but a strategic business goal.

hot card file

Retail Decisions maintains the APACS database of lost and stolen cards that it administers in the UK. (That's approaching 5 million cards that are either separated from their rightful owners or delinquent in some way.) It makes it available on-line, in real time to its retailers in any retail environment, providing the industry 'hot card' file. If you're paying at Sainsbury's or Tesco for example, a link to Retail Decisions' application of the hot card file automatically checks your card when it is presented as a way to pay for your shopping. This check is completed before the card is accepted, and it stops an average of 210,000 attempted card frauds every year, preventing an estimated £50 million of card fraud.

In the self-service environment, there is simply no excuse for not using this type of hot card file, which already checks 1.1 billion payments every year. The ability to use it is not affected by the fact that the card number has been typed in on a web page or entered using a telephone keypad.

It does, however, put stress on your application to use this in the self-service sector. Any demand for on-line-checking needs to be able to return a result inside a predetermined level of time. But with e-commerce systems scaling by around 30 per cent a month in some cases, this response time has to be monitored and upgrades have to be carried out well ahead of time.

If, during busy periods, you are unable to perform this simple process, then it's the equivalent of turning away customers because you don't know whether they are good customers or not. The loss of business is substantial. The loss of customer confidence in your systems may be as large.

In the future, more transaction-based card authentication will be designed especially for these platforms. Card Express is Retail Decisions' model for this market. It uses the sort of transaction-processing power that has been available for banking applications to provide real-time authentication for high-volume environments – and to make the transaction data available to the retailer. This is using one system to solve a fraud problem – but then to use the sort of information that solving that problem generated to feed back to the retailer and improve customer service. There's no need to build two applications when one will do!

rules and regulations

Simple business rules can be built into that application layer. They won't eliminate fraud, but for self-service they provide hard boundaries to your vulnerable areas. For example, there may be some rules for the type of transactions you are willing to process for certain foreign cards, or for certain issuers, or for certain delivery addresses (PO boxes come to mind). Self-service imposes a strict discipline on whether you accept these orders, because there is less opportunity for human error or for criminals to 'manipulate' the system.

knowledge-based systems and neural technology

While the hot card file is fine for combating fraud on cards that have already been stolen and reported and the rules impose a useful discipline, they don't handle the problem of fraud based on cards that haven't been stolen or aren't in high-risk categories – as, for example, in the two stories that started this chapter. This type of fraud isn't immediately apparent. However, it is possible to design systems that will combat it by matching the spending patterns of the customer to the recent spending patterns on that card.

The advantage of knowledge based systems is that they are controllable – as well as being used to disallow some fraudulent transactions, they might also be used as part of a retailer's self-service engine to do credit-scoring. This can help to create a managed environment for high-price goods, but it can also help to proactively manage your risk. If we accept that total elimination of all risk is not possible, we're then thinking about which risks it is appropriate to take and perhaps wanting to adjust that decision on a regular basis. That's what the neural technology used by a company like Retail Decisions can provide.

For fraud purposes, the card issuer also installs its own knowledge-based systems to analyse transactions before they are authorised.

Already, two-thirds of card issuers are using them, and the longer these systems are used, the better they become.

The systems, known also as 'neural networks', work in the same way as the human brain. They take real-world events and match them to an existing pattern that has been built up from the customer data that they already possess. Any transactions that don't seem to match – for example, sudden large payments, a burst of activity, transactions at odd times or with unexpected merchants – are flagged and can be queried.

A knowledge-based system does not work by pre-defined 'rules'. Like a child, it learns 'by experience'. On the one hand, this means that it can achieve higher standards of accuracy than a system that relies on inflexible rules (because you can never write enough rules to cater for every occurrence). It also makes the systems incredibly fast and means that they are constantly improving, taking time to come to peak efficiency.

On the other hand, a knowledge-based system will never be 100 per cent effective. Just as we sometimes mis-read a word, so a neural network will occasionally mis-read a transaction – as a customer, you may already have been asked to call your credit-card issuer while in a shop to confirm your identity. This procedure can err on the side of caution in a retail environment where there is some scope for customer interaction and the opportunity to explain to the customer what's going on. In a self-service situation though, there is no chance to do this. There is no mechanism yet to 'call the customer' and confirm an identity, so using this as an arbiter of which transactions are 'suspicious' would inevitably mean turning away some legitimate business. It's up to you to work out whether this would do more harm than good.

The ultimate arbiter of whether a neural scoring system works or not is the breadth and the quality of its information. Here also technology has made a huge difference. Take for example the eFalcon consortium, a six-year-old neural analysis tool developed specifically for the CNP market, which scores transactions based on hundreds of variables. It's the largest consortium of its type in the world. To run this type of analysis, you don't need to look at thousands of transactions, you need to look at millions.

SET and the electronic wallet

There are two main devices for payment on the Internet: SSL, or more completely, the secure sockets layer, or SET (secure electronic transactions).

SSL is the *de facto* standard for transactions from web sites, but it's a standard that has a fundamental problem: it doesn't authenticate an identity. Using SSL, the messages between vendor and purchaser are encrypted – the exact strength of the encryption depends on your location and the version of SSL used. In this way it protects legitimate customers from having their credit-card data read by a third party and inspires consumer trust, as the retailer can point to an exact measure of how secure the card number is.

While this might satisfy the honest consumer, it is also satisfactory for the dishonest one. SSL does not involve any authentication of the customer's identity. It works just as well for stolen credit card numbers as safe ones.

This may not be too serious a risk. If, for example, you are delivering physical goods, you have a cardholder's address and can do a more complete credit check before you ship. In the event of fraud, you also have a delivery address which can at least form the start of any fraud enquiry.

However, many self-service purchases on the web are not physical – and, increasingly, this will be the case for all businesses. If you are a supermarket, then part of your value is selling groceries but it might be an excellent business opportunity to sell services – for example, on-line recipes, or membership of a wine club. The groceries can use an off-line card check and increased security, but anything delivered on-line doesn't provide that opportunity.

This applies to many more devices than we might imagine. Computer software and services in the future will undoubtedly be delivered using a broadband computer network. Pay-as-you-go content such as digital television or on-line magazines and newspapers are also susceptible to CNP fraud, even though SSL is used.

SET is an attempt, jointly developed by Visa and MasterCard, to eliminate this problem by making that secure link between the merchant and the customer one side of a 'triangular' transaction. In a SET transaction, the merchant passes details of the customer back to the acquirer (although without the details of the transaction). The acquirer authenticates the user and passes a software 'token' to the user, who can use that token to complete the transaction with the merchant.

This all happens on-line. It inspires confidence in all three parties, while respecting the privacy of the transaction between the merchant and the customer. At the moment, SET has proved to be more difficult to implement practically, because of the inertia of the payment regime in place (with one billion cards in use worldwide, it's a lot of customer behaviour to change in a short time). In trials it has also proved difficult to scale – if the time taken to complete a transaction is more than a few seconds, the customer will walk away. And because the customer has to be sitting at the PC on which his or her personal encrypted information is stored, it's not flexible. So far, SET has proved to be a business risk that merchants and acquirers are loathe to take, although architecturally its security is not in doubt.

prepayment

One possible way around this problem is prepayment – making the user store value with you and spend from an 'account'. This is

me-t@iling

currently under research for so-called micropayments – the sort of payments that are not practical or economic to make using a credit card. Imagine you want to buy a single newspaper by self-service. In the real world (at least in the USA), you drop change into a streetside newspaper bin which unlocks the door so you can take your paper. On the Internet, the need for a similar service is obvious.

Many approaches are under research, but one of the highest-profile is Compaq's 'Millicent' technology. The customer stores value in an 'electronic wallet' – a software wallet which can be reloaded using a secure credit-card payment (which can, of course, be authenticated off-line). On the net, if the customer sees something that needs a tiny payment – a news story or a share price – (or just wants to use a site where these tiny payments – as low as a thousandth of a penny – are automatically deducted), then the payments come from the electronic wallet in a secure, pre-authenticated transaction, with no waiting.

The problem with micropayments is that they are, essentially, a new currency and one that you have to buy ahead of time. Until there are enough vendors who will use micropayments and who have committed to one technology standard, then forcing this security technology on to customers is a great way to put them off.

stored value

Perhaps a better route to secure transactions will be through the 'chip card' – the next generation of the traditional credit card. Already in use in much of Europe, these cards on which a tiny silicon chip is used instead of the insecure, data-poor stripe will soon replace the UK's traditional magnetic-stripe credit and debit cards.

This will immediately have a dramatic effect on card fraud. Whereas a mag-stripe card is relatively easy to counterfeit, a chip card is almost impossible to copy, because the chip actively identifies the card as genuine. In the self-service environment, this would help to reduce fraud in vending machines or in any application – such as a self-scanning device – where the card is read without the retailer being present. Counterfeit cards cost the UK £27 million in 1998. Chip card verification can also include extra methods of establishing identity – the card can store data on a customer's fingerprint or retinal scan, not just a PIN. The technology exists to do this today, but obviously it will demand a great deal of development to make it practical.

Chip cards are also a key element in the SET transaction: by providing their own level of authentication, they can make an electronic wallet more practical and easier to use. For the next five years at least, a smart-card reader will be a novelty on a home PC and unavailable on a mobile phone, so chip cards are a long way from being pervasive, and, if you wait for them, you might wait too long.

One area where chip cards will contribute to the success of self-service is that of stored value. Because chip cards can store value internally, whether that value is hard cash or inherent in a loyalty scheme, they provide a secure payment method. Yet consumers have been slow to take to pilots of the Mondex and Visa Cash cards, preferring the known convenience of cash for now.

But a similar 'stored value' application has already changed self-service completely in one application – the phonecard. A BT card for use in its phone boxes is a smart card with stored value. In trials, BT has allowed phonecard users to pay for car parking using value from the card, but, for this to become practical, BT would require a loosening of the regulatory framework surrounding card use.

chip cards and loyalty

Stored-value cards have a disadvantage in the self-service environment. Although they do not expose the merchant to credit risk, they don't identify the customer, and so we lose some of the precious marketing information we need. But if a chip card can be used as a loyalty card and store value too, then the customer can be

me-t@iling

identified, the transaction made secure, and the card offered as a convenient way to pay for self-service applications.

This has been trialled by both ICL and Groupe Bull. So far, in limited pockets, it has been successful. But it relies on a three-part deal: an established loyalty scheme encompassing more than one retailer, customer acceptance of stored value as a way to pay, and point-of-sale terminals that can accommodate this application. With 610,000 POS terminals in the UK, this might be a scheme that's just too grand at present.

automating simple errors

Whereas some risk arises from fraud and some from customer disputes, there's an area of self-service which gives rise to many disputed credit-card transactions: incorrect card details. There are also some schemes for reducing this problem — some of them surprising.

Traditionally, call centres have taken and rekeyed credit card details. Touch-tone recognition is one way to avoid rekeying errors but transactions are still vulnerable to user keying errors — which is why some IVR applications read back the credit-card number.

You will remember that we looked at Speechworks, the company that produces software capable of recognizing a vocabulary of words for self-service phone transactions. Speechworks has most often used this for basic information or booking but has found that when users read their credit-card number into the phone, even allowing for small recognition errors, it is more accurate than rekeying.

Several e-commerce sites have also alighted on the technology called 'one-click' by Amazon. If customers have the confidence to supply a credit-card number that Amazon keeps securely, then on each page there's a 'one-click' button. So you browse for a book, click a single button and it's ordered. There's no need to re-enter any card details. The card has been authenticated for the last transaction, and this transaction is approved before the book is shipped.

There's a danger that, when we talk technology, we lose sight of the business driver behind managing risk. This is not a technology problem. It is fundamentally a financial burden. And this financial burden will get a lot worse if you don't manage it. If a CNP transaction is fraudulent, then the issuer can make the merchant – that's you as a retailer – liable for that fraud – a 'chargeback' in other words. If chargebacks exceed 1 per cent of your value or 2.5 per cent of your volume for credit-card transactions and are sustained for a specified period, then you might lose merchant status. As far as the acquiring bank and the issuer are concerned, you have become a fraud risk.

To put some figures on this, at the beginning of March, 2000, Europay, which is responsible for the administration of the MasterCard brand in Europe, put in a scheme of chargebacks for e-commerce as follows: in the third month that chargebacks were over 1 per cent, the fine would be $10,000 per week. But by the sixth month, that's $25,000 every week. In month eight, it's $50,000 every week. In month ten, the merchant is terminated. Similar fines and structures apply for Visa payments.

While e-commerce is superficially becoming a marketing success, its great failure remains concealed: chargeback rates in the USA are reportedly topping 4 per cent. In Europe, they may be as high as 8 per cent.

This is a staggering failure. In normal transactions, the losses are around 0.1 per cent, a multiplier of 80. So the next time an e-commerce site tells you that giving your credit-card details on the net is no riskier than giving them in a restaurant, you know that retailer is talking about consumer risk. From the merchant's standpoint, this is a huge, unreported black hole.

To keep pace with the success that they have had in marketing and

me-t@iling

building ways for users to shop, the dot-coms have to build systems that protect honest users from the effects of fraud – and ultimately protect their own businesses. This is where the traditional retailers have the advantage. Fraud management is a long-standing discipline, the rules of which need to be applied as much in the self-service world as outside it.

Everyone can be susceptible to CNP fraud and the more successful your business, the more likely it becomes – if every opportunity isn't taken to suppress it. And the frauds may only come to light too late. For example, in the early days of BT Cellnet's prepay phone scheme, users discovered that credit cards used to recharge the prepay cards were not being authorised. The scale of the CNP fraud was massive, and, by the time it was discovered, the 'free' calls that unscrupulous users had made had been completed. On the other hand, everyone has the opportunity to fix these problems. BT Cellnet is now a customer of Retail Decisions.

In the self-service environment, all the retail innovation in the world does not mean that the existing risks vanish. If anything, they intensify.

CHAPTER 8
where do we go from here?

For the customer, self-service is about taking action, it's about taking responsibility, it's about making decisions. That's doubly the case for retailers. There's no point to this book if it just makes you think, 'gosh', or worse, 'so what?' Doing nothing and hoping that the issue will go away aren't options. The examples, the cautionary tales and the business successes suggest ten lessons that can be learned.

1. if you're not early, you're late

Half-hearted self-service simply doesn't work. Unless it delivers benefits comparable to those from your traditional sales channel, you look as if you're penalising customers for wanting the power to run their own lives. This is not an attractive message to send. A real commitment to the sales channel involves a fundamental reappraisal of where the value lies in your business model. This isn't something that can be done in an afternoon. On the other hand, it's not something that can be done over six months, because in six months it may already be too late, so it's going to be a pain.

2. automate the processes

The contraction of the self-service process isn't enough on its own to ensure success, but without it you're certainly guaranteeing failure. If you are looking at your business processes and wondering how they can be translated into the self-service model – in effect, how to build this machine – then perhaps you are not looking deeply enough at how it is constructed. We've seen how a 40-stage mortgage process can be translated for self-service. We've seen it

me-t@iling

handle 50,000 suppliers for two of the world's largest retailers. We've even seen it used in the courts.

Self-service has to be automatic. That's its benefit. When you lose that focus, you lose the value of the project.

Is your retail process really more complex than that? Probably not. The difference is that you may not be able to plug into the parts of your systems that it's essential to find. For example, you want to give overseas buyers the exact price they will have to pay for goods when they are delivered, including duty, customs and international shipping charges, when they access your intranet. You can't do it, so you give the customer the basic price, plus a message that there will be some unspecified additional cost. That's what nine out of ten companies do today.

But this information is not only available, it's possible to integrate it with your application in days. In the UK, there's a company called ISM that does exactly that for traditional retailers who have never had this challenge before. The difference is that, before, you're giving customers internal data, afterwards, you are offering them a service. One is no more work than the other – it's as easy to get it right, as to get it wrong.

3. **be strict on yourself**
Badly designed self-service applications get found out, because you're opening your internal processes to your customers. Ask the simple questions. Does this take longer to use? Does this offer what most people want from us? Are we offering services that nobody else does? Are we stymied for internal political reasons, or for genuine business reasons? And, as David Berger of Callcentric says, use the service yourself. If it's no good, be prepared to admit it, because in self-service you can't hide.

4. **customer first**
Most companies still put the process ahead of the customer. So it's

someone buying insurance, not someone protecting their belongings – which might lead to a number of other services that can be offered on the back of the basic transaction. Or it's a phone call, so it uses the call centre's set of rules, as opposed to the web site's set of rules for dealing with customers. At the other end of the phone line or the Internet connection, your customers don't make a distinction. Why should you?

A basic example: if there's a delay answering an e-mail enquiry, do your customers get a message saying, 'Sorry, we're still working on it, we'll have the answer as soon as possible'? If not, then why not? That's the message you should offer to people who are stuck in the telephone queue.

5. be like the dot-comers

Be prepared to get it wrong. Don't get it wrong all the time, but if you never make a mistake then you never do anything right either. It's impossible to predict with certainty what to do in this environment. Some of it is well-known, tried and tested technology, the sort of application that retailers feel happy with. Some is untried, untested, and might not work too well. But, unless it is given the opportunity to fail, it will never succeed.

6. measure success and failure

On the other hand, you've got to have a yardstick. Companies that get stuck in 'pilot purgatory', where their systems are forever being trialled to see if they will work, are guaranteed to get the answer that they won't. Waiting to see if your customers like the idea of self-service is like hanging around waiting for the love of your life to ask you out. If it happens, you've got more than you deserve. Make a target. Make someone responsible for achieving that target. Put a number on it – a percentage of business, a number of new customers. If that target isn't reached, try to measure why not, fix those problems and measure again. Do this every month. On the net, as we have seen, some companies are doing this every day. This is the standard in this market.

Invite a response. Self-service is a medium that invites immediate gratification, or otherwise. If there's no way for those customers to give feedback, then you have no idea what that response is.

Some customer response will be implicit. If your customers are prepared to get information from you using self-service, but won't complete the transaction, then they are either scared, confused or just not excited by the idea. But you don't know which one unless you ask them. Also, if you're not providing a service that your customers want, they won't necessarily let you know. They are self-service customers, and it's not their job to do that unless you make it worth their while.

7. **lead good customers, force bad ones**

This is about changing behaviour, not having your behaviour changed. Invite customers to try it once. Give them an instant incentive to try again a second time. It could be a discount, a free gift, a free service, or just an exceptional service that surprised them. Forcing your loss-making customers into self-service makes financial sense. It might also make sense to them. They might not think about your business very much, they might not be very committed to it. If that remains unchanged, then self-service either makes them cheaper to support, or, if it is a fast, easy-to-use service, it might make them more committed or more loyal.

But you need to pull and push with commitment. You need those resources that self-service frees to expand your business. If you don't make them available, no one will give them to you.

8. **involve everyone**

This isn't about simply designing one system and sticking it on the front of one operation. Self-service is a customer-support channel, it's a sales channel, it's a marketing channel. It's a security and privacy risk and a business development opportunity. It involves the IT function from day one — but it's not a technology problem. If all these disciplines aren't involved, then you're lessening the chances for success.

But also these disciplines have to be pushed together and forced — if necessary — to share power. Unless the marketing department shares the feedback from the web site, the customer support function doesn't work. Unless every channel to the customer is equally secure, then one channel will become a focus for fraud. No one 'owns' self-service any more than they 'own' the customers who might use it.

9. be prepared for success

Failure isn't good. Success can be worse. As we have seen, scalability in self-service is essential. If a community works with 1,000 customers, does it work with 100,000? If you can give real-time response to a self-service customer off-peak, can you do it at peak times? If you hit your five-year target inside one year (as Internet savings bank Egg did) do you have the budget to keep recruiting customers, and do you have the ability to keep expanding? If you invite your customers to come to you, and they turn up, it's too late to turn them away.

10. get the fundamentals right

In the words of one call-centre consultant, if you get it wrong, 'Pack up and stop embarrassing your customers'. A jerry-built self-service operation is a customer-loser, a security risk, a risk to your brand and a signal that whoever is running the business has no commitment to the future. If you attract fraud, then your competitors are beating their fraud problem by doing nothing. There seems to be no middle ground in any of the applications we have seen — either they fly, or they crash. Or they fly, then crash.

This is not an experiment.

If these are the tasks, then what can we say about the rewards of moving to self-service? The first is, in the words of one management

me-t@iling

consultant, 'that you get to keep your job'. Because, as we have seen, self-service retailing allows you to innovate and expand the products you offer quickly and to respond to new pressures and new markets in a creative way, it's a powerful tool to help you compete. But it's also a powerful tool for enabling others to grab your business on the cheap.

For example, Dell's idea that users could build their own computer on the Internet and then have exactly that computer built to order on the production line wasn't just a good idea – it was a method that allowed the company to innovate. Imagine that a new processor comes on to the market. Because of the way in which personal computers are made, that processor can just be slotted into the list of available options immediately stocks arrive – on the same day, it can be offered for sale on the company's web page or over the phone. While rival manufacturers in the mid-1990s were struggling to empty warehouses of obsolete computers that they had built, but failed to sell in time, Dell never had that problem, and, unless it changes its policy now, it never will.

Here are the advantages. First, every time new technology came to market, customers could go and pick it for themselves. Dell staff were not constantly firefighting to reduce the cost of inventory, which according to arch-rival Compaq at the time was costing Dell's competitors £50 per computer. Dell customers got what they wanted, because they could pick what they wanted, and it was always in stock, and always at that day's price.

Second, self-service will save you money. We've seen the impact that IVR has in the call centre, that the web has on overheads, and that devices like kiosks can have in terms of staff reduction – or, if the wind blows your way, staff redeployment to capitalise on expanding business opportunities. But if you do this just to save cash, you're running a huge risk. Let's say that instead of making your business cheaper to run, it makes expansion less expensive.

Third, it gives you a happy customer — ideally, many happy customers, who feel empowered to make choices and to reap the benefits of those choices.

Fourth, it gives you a route into the future. New retail channels like television and the Internet are, as we saw, overwhelmingly based on self-service principles. You can take a business model that works on the net, and adapt it for television. You can take a model that works for IVR in a call centre and you can adapt it for the Internet. You can even take a web page and allow users to access it through a telephone. But, unless you have one of these models working, you're not at the starting line for any of them.

Fifth, it can tell you more about your customers than the day-to-day interactions that you are accustomed to. This is absolutely fundamental. In the UK, companies rarely put 'knowledge' or 'goodwill' on the balance sheet. You can argue that this is for a good reason, that any arbitrary figure carries little weight and fools nobody.

But knowledge of your customers and their willingness to come back to your retail business taken together are surely a much more accurate measure of the health of your business ten years from now than the value of your fixtures and fittings. Indeed, in another decade, many of these fixtures and fittings will be liabilities. It is vital to be able to second-guess your self-service customers and your traditional buyers alike. If you do that, you can upsell them. You can't second-guess them until you know what they like. So to upsell, you need to collect good data, and turn it into good information.

Every time your customers serve themselves, they identify themselves. They leave accurate and truthful information. This is not the case with traditional sales channels.

Sixth, you are protecting yourself from deflation. For the first time, retail products are getting cheaper. The 'race to the bottom' has already begun, and you're running in it. The pure markets that e-

me-t@iling

commerce encourages abhor a margin — but self-service leaves more of that margin in the retailer's hand, either on or off the net.

Finally, this is, in the consultant's argot, a 'zero-sum game'. People will not eat more food because it takes less time to buy it. They will not buy two computers because it took half the time to serve them, or make two telephone calls where one will do. But if you can serve them better, faster and cheaper, they'll buy your food, your computer or use your telephone handset and not your competitor's. It's not just the customers who can help themselves in the self-service revolution. The smart retailers can as well.